Additional Praise for
Memories of The Catskills

"Those were the days my friends!! Whatever your frame of reference of the 'Catskills' is—guest, staff member or 'just heard about the area' you will find Al Lesser's book a delight. Traveling down memory lane, while reading this sincere and heartwarming true story, brought back many wonderful memories. Al Lesser has given us a unique opportunity to go behind the scenes and learn how it all happened. I laughed, smiled, and also shed a few tears with the Lesser family. Whether one came from a smaller property, or a large one such as mine (Grossinger's), we all traveled the same road, perhaps with a few minor detours. Our ultimate destination was identical—Hospitality for the folks who vacationed with us. Next scheduled activity, READ *Memories of The Catskills.*"

Elaine Grossinger Etess
Grossinger's Hotel

"*Memories of The Catskills* by Alvin Lesser is a candid and charming memoir about the rise and fall of the 'Borscht Belt.' Lesser Lodge, a small hotel where the author spent the better part of his childhood, lies at the center of this heartfelt tale. Anecdotes in the book range from Kirk Douglas's father calling out 'cash for clothes' and Jerry Lewis appearing in the Catskill hotels, to matzoh balls, fried food, and boyhood memories of catching fish bare-handed in a stream. The spirit of life itself is captured and offered up on these pages."

Robin Reinach
New York, NY

"Anyone who ever set foot in the Catskill Mountains during the halcyon days of the Borscht Belt has precious memories that with the passage of time may begin to slowly fade. Anyone who never did truly missed something special. Fortunately for all of us, Alvin Lesser put his in a wonderfully crafted book that helps keep those memories alive.

"Alvin Lesser's genius for weaving humorous (I'm talking belly laughs here) and tearful memories in rapid fire succession (his style is reminiscent of Bill Bryson's, 'In a Sunburned Country') into a first person grand tale of a bygone era, takes the reader along on a delightful journey back to those golden days. If I close my eyes I'm at once a kid again reliving all the glory of those magical moments. After reading his book I am sure you will feel the same way too."

George Sewitt
Highland Mills, NY
Seasonal guest and camper

"Alvin Lesser's book, *Memories of The Catskills*, takes you back to the days when the Sullivan County Summer was thriving; when the roads were curb-to-curb with cars, and the days were filled with games and picnics, swimming and visiting; when the nights were filled with plenty of food and soon-to-be-famous entertainers. It's a day that's long gone, but one that lives in a lot of memories. How fortunate that Lesser has graciously shared his memories with us; he's captured the spirit and the harmony that brought the Catskills to life."

Carol Montana
Editor, The Catskill Chronicle

"Alvin Lesser's *Memories of The Catskills* is more than just memorabilia. Famous stars of yesteryear came to entertain in the 'Borscht Belt' at Lesser Lodge. The Lodge survived the depression era and then flourished during the years of economic recovery and growth. Not just the story of the Lesser family, but the warmth of people who made others welcome by providing a respite which made them all family— entertainers and guests alike. Five stars for this one."

Clark Isaacs
Clark's Eye on Books

"*Memories of The Catskills* by Alvin Lesser is a cordial and funny gem of a memoir. The author's humorous tone is matched by whimsical sketches that are sprinkled throughout the book. Photographs of Lesser Lodge and the many characters that populated this small hotel evoke a nostalgic appreciation of years gone by. The author's voice is matter-of-fact and filled with gratitude. Yet, this reader couldn't help getting the feeling that Alvin Lesser was winking—just a little!"

Richard Epstein
New York, NY

"*Memories of The Catskills* is a poignant reminder of simpler times for residents of New York City who escaped to the mountains for a week or two to unwind. It was a rite of summer for many of us, and one that was done repeatedly over the years. This book does an excellent job of describing a time and a place that is difficult for people today to appreciate; read it and be transported back to simpler times."

David Budlin
Valrico, FL

"Alvin Lesser offers valuable reports, photos, and graphics that describe the daily life of a medium-sized Catskills hotel. This is a rare opportunity to learn how these quintessential family-run resorts were managed. The chronological narrative of new buildings, pool, dam, lake, entertainment casino, children's day camp, and remodeled rooms takes us from the early 1920s boarding home to the destruction by fire in 1963 of a hotel that could hold 270 guests. With its hand-drawn map and detailed descriptions, Lesser's book makes us feel like we were living that resort life over a half century earlier."

Phil Brown
Northeastern University
Distinguished Professor of
Sociology and Health Sciences

"New York's 'Borscht Circuit' is second only to Hollywood, CA as the birthplace of a distinctly American entertainment. And just as with Hollywood, so too with the Borscht Circuit, the best stories are often found when one looks beyond the famous people with their bigger-than-life personas to the everyday characters that actually made the place and gave it its sense of style.

"Alvin Lesser's *Memories of The Catskills* is a book about just such people. It is filled with *their* stories as seen first through the eyes of an innocent but mischievous child, then through those of a young adult struggling to make his way in the world, and finally from the standpoint of a returning WWII veteran who has seen humanity at both its best and its worst. It is witty, humorous and insightful, but somehow never overtly sentimental.

"Memories of The Catskills tells the story of a small but prominent Borscht Circuit hotel: The Lesser Lodge. What one expected when one visited a hotel in the Catskills was to be thoroughly entertained, to escape the daily grind of life, and to eat heartily until you reached the near-bursting point. And so it is with Alvin Lesser's *Memories of The Catskills*. It will thoroughly entertain you, it will open to you a world that seems today completely fresh and new, and it will fill you with laughter and pure delight."

Don Sucher
Peterborough, NH
Former Catskill Mountain
resort musician[1]

"What a wonderful gift to all of us with faded recollection of a bygone era. Let the flood gates of forgotten memories swing open with each flip of the page. This book is much more than a collection of charming stories. This book is an anthology of cultural artifacts. Wouldn't it be wonderful if all of history could be recorded in such a warm, heartfelt and personal manner?"

Dr. Mitchell S. Cohen
Clarke Summit, PA
Former Catskill Mountain resident

"Cross Woody Allen's *Radio Days* with *Dirty Dancing* and you will have a sense of the world that *Memories of The Catskills* recreates: slapstick, shot through with sentimentality and the fundamentals of Borscht Belt humor: irony, acceptance, and a hearty appetite for all life has to offer."

Christine Roberts
Santa Barbara, CA

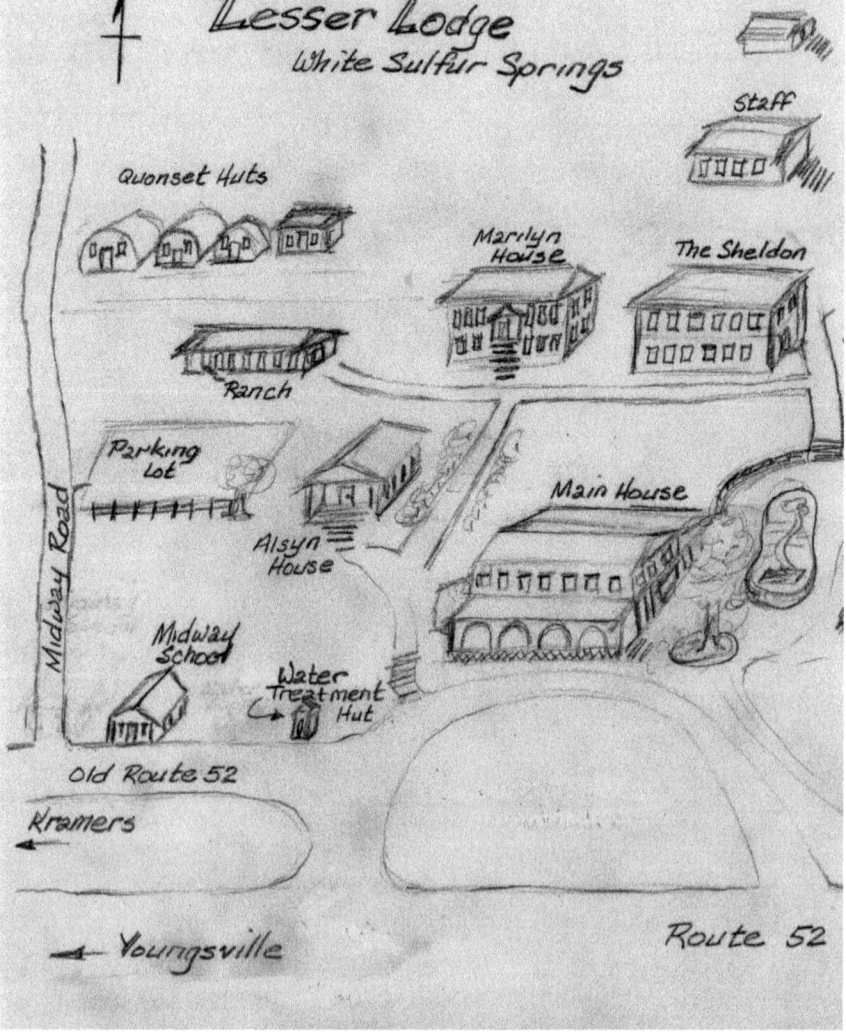

N

Lesser Lodge
White Sulfur Springs

Staff

Quonset Huts

Marilyn House

The Sheldon

Ranch

Parking Lot

Main House

Alsyn House

Midway Road

Midway School

Water Treatment Hut

Old Route 52

Kramers

Youngsville

Route 52

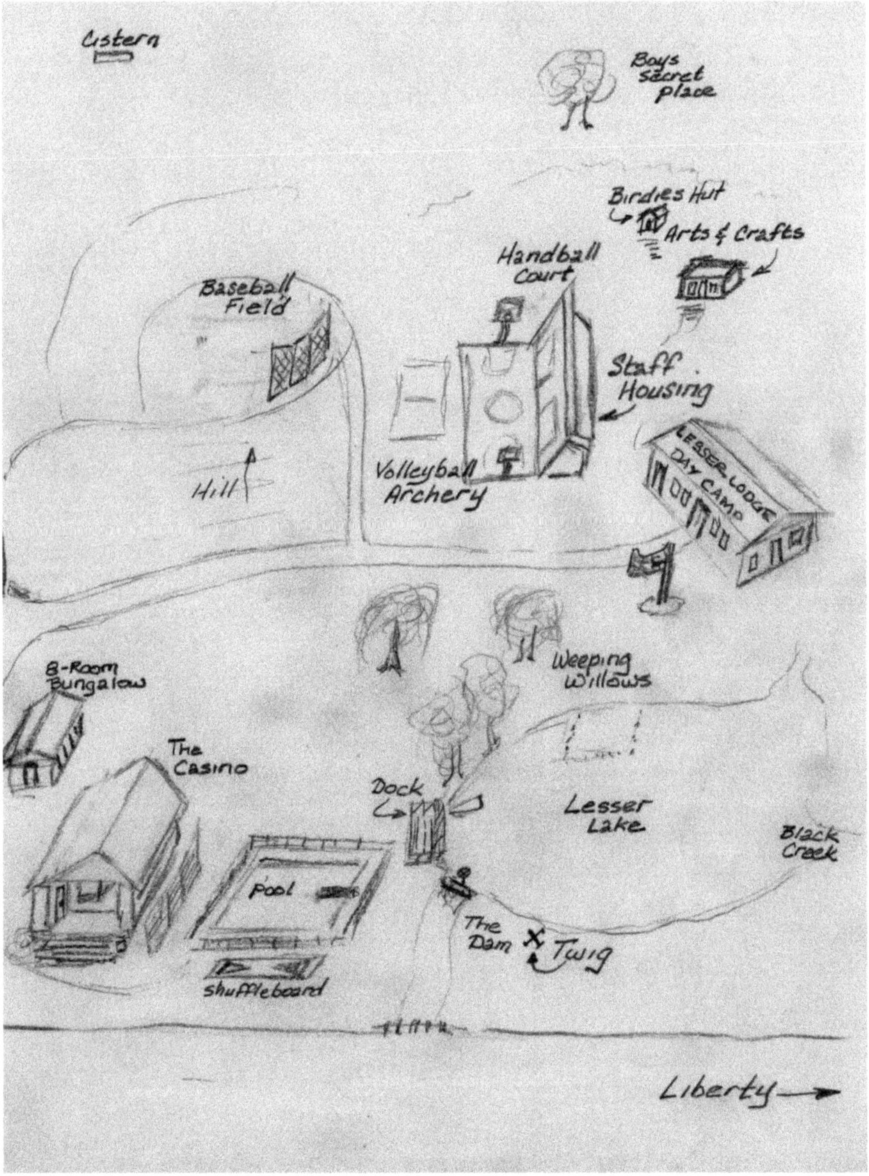

Cistern
Boys secret place
Birdies Hut
Arts & Crafts
Handball Court
Baseball Field
Staff Housing
LESSER LODGE DAY CAMP
Volleyball Archery
Hill
8-Room Bungalow
Weeping Willows
The Casino
Dock
Lesser Lake
Black Creek
Pool
The Dam
Twig
shuffleboard
Liberty

Memories of The Catskills

The Making of a Hotel

Alvin L. Lesser

Foreword by John Conway
Sullivan County Historian

Published in the United States

GSL Galactic Publishing
Indianapolis, IN
QPSEP@aol.com

ISBN: 978-0-9993229-4-9 (Hardcover)
ISBN: 978-0-9680034-1-7 (eBook)

1 2 3 4 5 6 7 8 9

Edited by
Don and Jan Sucher,
Rita Hupp and Carol Montana

Illustrations by
Charlie Lewallen

Cover design by
Kathryn Marcellino

FOREWORD

By John Conway

Tourism in Sullivan County dates back to at least 1840, when fishermen who had learned of the bounty of the region's waters through the writings of Alfred B. Street, Charles Fenno Hoffman, and others began to travel to the area to try their luck. By 1846, there were enough summer boarders arriving at White Lake that John Beekman Finlay constructed a hotel specifically for their benefit. Finlay's hotel, the name of which has been lost to time, was not successful, but the Mansion House, built nearby by David Barton Kinne in 1848, was, and White Lake became the county's first summer resort.

By 1890, when the tanning and timber industries that had dominated the region's economy for so long had faded from the scene and three railroads provided accessibility and promotion, Sullivan County began a period of prosperity historians today call the Silver Age. Hundreds of hotels and thousands of farmhouses provided accommodations to those looking to escape the oppressive heat of nearby overpopulated cities, and Sullivan County gained prominence as a vacation destination.

When the Silver Age ended in 1915, the county underwent a transition. By this time, most of the hotels were struggling or had closed down. Many were purchased by Jewish immigrants moving into the mountains from New York City and Brooklyn. These ambitious neophyte owners not only breathed new life into their hotels, but expanded and modernized them.

This transition period was marked by several phenomena. The clapboard-sided Victorian hotels of the previous era were replaced by distinctive stucco-covered structures with Palladian windows and often elaborate parapets. This unique style, called *Sullivan County Mission*, became a hallmark of the region during the 1920s and '30s.

Since the railroad had declined in significance— the peak year for passenger travel on the O&W Railway had been in 1913—and the automobile provided enhanced accessibility, the summer hotels no longer had to be located close by the train stations.

As providing entertainment for the guests became more and more obligatory, talent-laden social staffs became the norm. Some hotels had thirty or forty members on their entertainment staffs, and future greats like Moss Hart, Dore Schary, Don Hartman, Danny Kaye, Jerry Lewis, Robert Merrill, Jan Peerce, Jan Murray, Red Buttons, Sid Caesar, and Van Johnson got their starts on the social staffs of Catskill resorts.

By 1940, a new period of prosperity now called the Golden Age had begun, and by the middle of the next decade, the *New York Times* was reporting that there were 538 hotels in Sullivan County, along with 1,000 rooming houses and 50,000 bungalows. The hotels included two of the most famous resorts in the world, Grossinger's in Ferndale and the Concord at Kiamesha Lake. But the story of the Golden Age is not so much the story of the behemoths such as these as it is the story of the hundreds of small and medium-sized hotels in places like Mountaindale, Fallsburg, Hurleyville, and Livingston Manor. The story of the Golden Age is the story of places like the Lesser Lodge in White Sulphur Springs.

White Sulphur Springs had a rich tradition as a resort community and had developed as a Silver Age tourist destination despite the fact that it was not served directly by the railroad. The mineral springs for which the community literally got its name played a major role in that development. Thousands of vacationers came each summer to partake of its heavily promoted curative properties. White Sulphur Springs was also one of the first communities in Sullivan County to host professional prizefighters training for upcoming bouts. Early headliners such as Frank Moran and Battling Levinsky set up training camps there as early as 1916.

The presence of the springs notwithstanding, White Sulphur Springs was never home to a large hotel by Sullivan County standards, but a number of small- to medium-sized hotels were located there, and in the era of the automobile, these hotels helped fuel the economies, not just in their own community but in nearby Liberty as well, where visitors regularly walked Main Street and patronized the businesses there.

These hotels lured the same vacationers back year after year and treated them like members of the family. Unlike the big hotels, these smaller establishments were not able to offer their guests continual entertainment, no matter how hard they might try and that worked to the benefit of the local communities. When these smaller hotels began to close down in the mid- to late '60s, the local economy took a direct hit. When the Golden Age ended, it was the demise of these smaller hotels that hurt the area the most.

With each passing year, there are fewer folks who remember this era. That's why efforts like this book are so important and so vital to preserving memories of a time that will likely never be duplicated.

John Conway
Sullivan County Historian*

---

*John Conway was born and raised in Sullivan County, New York, and educated at Georgia Institute of Technology in Atlanta, Georgia. He has been the Sullivan County Historian since 1993 and an adjunct professor at State University of New York at Sullivan since 1999.

He is the author of 8 books about various aspects of the Catskills. John wrote a weekly column on local history for the *Times Herald-Record* newspaper for more than twelve years beginning in 1987 and currently writes a similar column for the *Sullivan County Democrat*. He was a contributor for the latest edition of the *Encyclopedia of New York State*.

By Myrna Katz Frommer
and Harvey Frommer

Memories of the Catskill is guaranteed to bring back memories for anyone who ever spent any time up the "Mountains" as it used to be called. It brought back memories for us, but not so much of idyllic youthful summers as of one particular summer: 1989 soon after we had signed a contract with Harcourt Brace Jovanovich to write a book about the renowned "Borscht Circuit."

On a windy day in early March of that year, we headed up Route 17 to begin our research. The plan was to write a straightforward historical account about the birth and growth of a resort region some 90 miles north of New York City. Our first stop was at the Nevele Hotel in the little town of Ellenville. We spoke to a couple of waiters, the owner -- Julie Slutsky, and a guy who was playing in the band. A small start but enough to tell us this was a story that would not be told by us, but by those who were sharing their memories with us. There was no improving on the style, the voice, the particular turn of phrase – the Catskill ethos. Through the months that followed, as we visited hotels and bungalow colonies, from the small and modest to the grand and palatial, our original sense was confirmed. By Labor Day, we had interviewed nearly 100 people. A few months later, we handed in a finished manuscript: "It Happened in the Catskills, An Oral History in the

Words of Busboys, Bellhops, Guests, Proprietors, Comedians, Agents and Others Who Lived It."

Somehow, however, we missed out on a great story: Alvin Lesser and the Lesser Lodge. We say this with a touch of regret – it would have made for a terrific entry in our book. But happily, this warm, evocative, poignant and at the same time hilarious story is now told in these pages from its beginnings in 1923 to the sad day some four decades later when Lesser Lodge closed.

In 1989, the decline of the Catskill resort phenomenon was just a dim cloud over the horizon. In 2012, it's virtually gone. But it remains in the memories of those who lived it and in wonderful books like this one. It fills you up like a brimming bowl of matzoh-ball soup. You can't get enough.

---

* The husband and wife team of Myrna Katz Frommer and Harvey Frommer are well-known oral historians and co-authors of critically acclaimed works including: *It Happened in the Catskills*; *It Happened in Brooklyn*; and *Growing Up Jewish in America*. Professors of oral history in the Liberal Studies program at Dartmouth College, they are lecturers and prolific travel writers whose articles on national and international destinations have appeared in *The New York Times, Newsday, The L.A. Times, Redbook, Golf Digest* and others.

Harvey Frommer is also a noted sports journalist and the author of 41 books on sports including the autobiographies of legends Nolan Ryan, Tony Dorsett, and Red Holzman.

Alvin L. Lesser

My son asked me to write the book *Memories of The Catskills.* I immediately replied with an adamant "No." I told him I had spent one-and-a-half years writing our first book, *Basic Accounting Simplified,* and I had no intention of leaving my sedentary life playing bridge, tennis, and other pleasurable things. He said, "But Dad, I would like to know what you did in your youth and how the Lesser Lodge was built." That got to me. Now that I'm going to be ninety and am "middle aged," I told my son I would write the book. Better now than when I'm old.

Much of my early biography is included in the pages of this book. During the summers I aided my parents in running the Lesser Lodge and I had the winters free to attend college and do as I wished. I helped my parents until 1963, when the main house was consumed by fire.

During 1942, I attended New York University for one semester, majoring in accounting. It was at this point that the United States Army decided the war could not be won unless "I led the charge." I spent the major part of my army career fighting through France and Germany. I went through many harrowing experiences during the war that I will more fully discuss in my next book, tentatively titled "Me and the Other Heroes of World War II."

My division, the 71st Infantry, liberated a concentration camp named Gunskirchen Lager.[1] It is hard for me to comprehend the inhumanity of man. I saw hundreds of people whose thighs were the size of my wrist. While I was at the concentration camp I saw a group of soldiers who had captured two SS Troopers. They said they were going to take them to headquarters. After shots were heard at a distance, the soldiers returned. I doubt if they even knew where headquarters was located.

On that day I happened to be on guard duty and my job was to be sure that no one entered a large German food supply building located near the concentration camp. A large group of the pathetic, starving prisoners approached me and one of them, a Frenchman, kept repeating the words "Juif, Juif." Of course, I realized he was saying, "Jew, Jew." I opened the door of the building and waved them in. I would rather have been court-martialed than let these suffering people go hungry.

As the war was ending, I was on guard duty. When on guard duty you almost invariably are alone. A group of German soldiers approached me, waving white flags, and shouting "surrender." Soon there were hordes and hordes of German soldiers joining the first group who had surrendered. There were literally thousands and thousands of soldiers around me surrendering *en masse.* Can you imagine all those Germans surrendering to a Jew? The truth is the German soldiers would rather surrender to an American Jew instead of to the Russians. I was awarded no medals for capturing thousands and thousands of German soldiers. Life is unfair.

I was doing a great deal of guard duty which entailed me being on guard for two hours and having four hours off. I didn't care for guard duty. As a matter of fact I disliked guard duty. I volunteered to become a member of the 71st Infantry boxing team and was accepted.

The boxing team was delightful duty. We could either train or go out walking and meeting German women. I chose the latter. All the boxers had to do was fight two times a week for three two-minute rounds. We used ten-ounce boxing gloves as contrasted to the six-ounce gloves used by professional boxers. When I was struck a vicious punch, it felt as if I was hit by a pillow. It was, indeed, delightful duty. While I fought, the only part of my body that tired was my arms. It wasn't easy holding up those ten-ounce boxing gloves.

This blissful life lasted until I was summoned to Division Headquarters in Augsburg, Germany. I was then informed I was a writer for the *Red Circle News*, the official newspaper of the 71st Division. Until the army was good enough to cruise me back to the United States, I was a staff writer for the *Red Circle News*.

After I was discharged, I took advantage of the Army's college program and graduated from New York University with a Bachelor of Science degree. My major was accounting and my minor was law. While attending college, on June 8, 1947, I married my wife, Evelyn. We have been married 63 years and my wife, 85 years of age, is still a beautiful woman.

During my first year in college I sold blood to medical institutions, which used it for patients needing transfusions. I received $30 each time I supplied blood. The last time I sold blood, the nurse apparently used a dirty needle in the process of extracting it. Both I and the recipient of the blood contracted infectious hepatitis, commonly referred to as jaundice.

Our family physician, Dr. Hirshkowitz, ordered me to spend a full month in the hospital, where I wasn't permitted to get out of bed. Incidentally, doctors operated, no pun intended, very differently from the way they do today. Doctors came to the home of the sick patient. They charged $3.00 a visit and they would frequently be forced to wait until the patient had the money to pay them. To my knowledge, there were no medical offices. When a person was ill, the doctor came to his or her home.

Being required to spend a month in the hospital was a mixed blessing. I had nothing to do other than to study accounting books and pamphlets. By the end of the month, I was so knowledgeable about accounting, I never received less than an "A" in all my accounting classes.

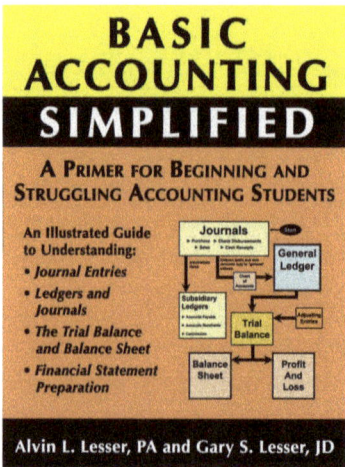

Years later, when I was 89 years of age, my son and I wrote a book, *Basic Accounting Simplified*. I did the writing and my son did the formatting and graphics.

BASIC ACCOUNTING SIMPLIFIED

A PRIMER FOR BEGINNING AND STRUGGLING ACCOUNTING STUDENTS

An Illustrated Guide to Understanding:
* Journal Entries
* Ledgers and Journals
* The Trial Balance and Balance Sheet
* Financial Statement Preparation

Journals · General Ledger · Subsidiary Ledgers · Trial Balance · Balance Sheet · Profit And Loss

Alvin L. Lesser, PA and Gary S. Lesser, JD

The book is being sold on the Internet and is doing very well.

In 1951, my wife and I bought our first home in Wantagh, New York, for $17,000. As time went by, we had the kitchen modernized. We removed the partition separating two rooms and made one large beautiful bedroom.

The original house came with a large living room which was located in back of our garage. Our next project was to break the wall separating the garage from the living room, and the result was we had a massive living room. We had a fireplace built and all the interior walls were wormy chestnut lumber.

Wormy chestnut is wood made from blighted chestnut trees, that is, from chestnut trees killed by boring worms that left small holes throughout the entire tree. In essence, when all the existing wormy chestnut wood boards have been used, there are no more available. Today, reclaimed wormy chestnut wood sells for about $15 a square foot.

We had purchased the wormy chestnut for approximately $2,000. Before we sold the house in 1988, we had the house appraised by two professional appraisers. Both valued the wormy chestnut at $40,000. After we sold our home, our neighbor, with whom we are still friendly, told us the purchaser of the house had all the wormy chestnut ripped out. They didn't sell the wood! They just ripped it out and placed it on the curb.

1241 Holly Road, Wantagh, NY

After my graduation, I rented an office in Deer Park, NY. Over time, I built up a large accounting practice. One of my clients named Glenndale Associates was in a real estate business which bought and sold commercial real estate all over the United States. I became involved in the business and passed the tests to become a real estate broker. Since the business consisted of only the buying and sale of land, it didn't take up a great deal of my time. I visited my accounting clients quarterly and had adequate help. So, I was able to handle both businesses.

In 1987, I sold my accounting practice and retired to Florida, where I joined the Boca Woods Country Club. After years of playing golf and a great deal of practice, I achieved the rank of "Duffer." Nowadays, I play bridge when I'm not playing with balls.

I hope you enjoy the book and have a few smiles and some laughs along the way.

[1] *The Seventy-First Came To Gunskirchen Lager*, E. Kieser KG, Druckerel u. Verlag, Augsburg (1945). The pamphlet was produced by the U.S. Army after they liberated a concentration camp in Austria called Gunskirchen Lager. The 71st arrived just days before VE day. The pamphlet recounts in detail and with very graphic photos the tragedy they found in the camp.

See, *http://www.jewishvirtuallibrary.org/jsource/ Holocaust/Gunskirchen.html*

ACKNOWLEDGMENT

Many individuals, relatives, and friends contributed to the book you hold in your hand. I value their friendship and assistance greatly.

I wrote this book primarily to describe the Catskills—what life was like there at a specific time and at a certain place.

I wish to express my great appreciation and deep gratitude to Don and Jan Sucher, Rita Hupp and Carol Montana for their expertise and editorial assistance; to John Conway, Sullivan County Historian, for writing such a compelling Foreword for the book; to Charlie Lewallen for her amusing and priceless illustrations; and to Kathryn Marcellino for her beautiful cover design. Additional thanks to Myrna and Harvey Frommer for writing an Introduction.

Special thanks to Mary Ann Drobysh-Berens of Mountainview Abstract Corporation in Monticello for her diligent research and gathering of the recorded deed history of the Lesser Lodge property, past and present; and to Dermot P. Dowd, a Civil Engineer with the Sullivan County Division of Public Works, for providing information and maps regarding the rerouting of Route 52 and the extension of Midway Road (formally Shingle Brook Road). This information is contained in Appendix B, The "Great Patent" and Other Deeds.

Additionally, I wish to express my deep appreciation and gratitude to Bernie and June Rader, Gloria Rader Katz, Mitchell S. Cohen, David and Paul

Auerbach, Norman Margolies, Jill Lesser, David Budlin, and Larry Schwalb for their assistance whenever called upon; to Alexis Bergman for providing engaging research and photographs; and to Christina Lucia Miles Reichenbaum for sharing some of her fondest childhood recollections (see The Beautiful Miles) and to her brother Jackie for the photographs and good times we all had together.

Special thanks to my son Gary for publishing this book and taking care of all the other components. Gary had the manuscript edited, prepared the footnotes and the appendices, collected the pictures and arranged the artwork.

Additional thanks to Eric Larson of CardCow.com for granting postcard permissions; and to Susan White of King Production Syndicate for granting the Katzenjammer Kids cartoon permission.

And finally, I would thank my magnificent wife, Evelyn, for everything. She deserves only the best. But, alas, had to settle for Lesser.

To all those mentioned and unmentioned who have provided pictures and refreshed my recollection, you know who you are, and I thank you too.

TABLE OF CONTENTS

MEMORIES OF THE CATSKILLS
THE MAKING OF A HOTEL

MY BIRTH (1922)

I was born on July 21, 1922. It seems the doctor who delivered me, Dr. Hirshkowitz, felt my birth was of no particular significance and did not file a birth certificate.

Apparently every cloud has a silver lining. My mother used to swear had I not been born at home, she would never have believed I was her son. I can't believe she said this about someone as sweet and lovable as I.

BUILDING OF THE PROPERTY (1923)

On July 17, 1923, when I was one year old, my parents, Joseph and Sarah Lesser, bought a house in White Sulphur Springs, New York. My parents made the decision on their own, without consulting me. White Sulphur Springs[2] is located between the towns of Liberty[3] and Youngsville in "the Catskills."

The property upon which the house was built was remarkably unsuited to the building of a hotel.[4] There were two levels where the construction took place. The main house and the eight-room bungalow were built on the lower level. The barn was on the upper level, where most of the future building took form.

*My sister Marilyn Auerbach in front
of barn (circa 1942)*

"THE CATSKILLS"

The term "Catskill Mountains" refers to the northern mountains in Ulster, Greene, and Orange Counties in upstate New York and the hotels (mostly gentile establishments) that operated there.[5]

On the other hand, the term "the Catskills" has come to mean specifically Sullivan County and the Borscht Belt hotels. The area was a popular vacation spot for New York City Jews from the 1920s through the 1960s.[6]

The terms "Borscht Belt" and "Jewish Alps" are colloquial terms that were used to describe the mostly now-defunct summer resorts of the Catskills.

Borscht is a soup made from beets that was popular among Slavic and Ashkenazi Jews who immigrated to the United States. It is frequently served cold with a boiled potato and a dollop of sour cream. As I found out many times, adding the sour cream to the borscht can be tricky and sometimes results in clothing turning red.

PURCHASE AND BUILDING OF PROPERTY (1923)

The purchase price of the property was $9,000, of which $2,500 was paid in cash and the balance by mortgage. The property consisted of the house, a barn, an eight-room bungalow, and approximately 50 acres of land. Also included on the purchase agreement were two single buggies, one heavy sleigh, one bay horse, five cows, 13 ducks, 250 chickens, 14 beds, and two small cots. [See Appendix B, The "Great Patent" and Other Deeds.]

Purchase Agreement (1923)

FRESH AIR (1923)

My parents bought the home in this region because my older brother, Seymour, had breathing problems. Because of its altitude (1,300 feet), it was generally believed that living in Liberty would help or cure those suffering from lung problems.[7]

Loomis Sanitarium,[8] a lung hospital, is located in Liberty. Thousands of patients were successfully treated there over the decades before the introduction of antibiotics. The sanitarium's remaining buildings are some of the County's greatest architectural treasures.

Loomis Sanitarium (1916). The back of the 1¢ post card reads: "Spending a few days in Liberty." [9]

JOSEPH LESSER [10] (1923)

When my parents realized they could make a living renting rooms during the summer season—July through August—my father began to temporarily leave his job as a sewing machine operator doing "piece work" (i.e., being paid by the amount of product he produced), and devote his time to hotel keeping. During this period, however, the hotel, or, more accurately, the "hotel to be" was not yet able to sustain itself financially. Thus my father continued to travel to New York City during the winter to augment the meager family income.

Each weekend my father returned to the hotel, generally traveling by rail. When he arrived he always had a copy of the *New York Times*. I was bitterly disappointed because the *Times* contained no comics. It made no difference that I was unable to read the comic strips; I enjoyed looking at the pictures.

My dad, Joseph Lesser, resting during the "off season"
(circa 1944)

My father was a stern man, but at times he could display a fine sense of humor, particularly when he had a drink or two.

SARAH LESSER [11] (1923)

My mother was 27 years old when my parents bought the house that was to become a hotel. My mother was short and heavy but she was strong. When I was 18 years old, she could walk behind me and lift me with ease. In contrast to my father who was stern, my mother was always cheerful.

Joseph and Sarah Lesser

Mom kept a kosher home because my Dad insisted on it. But when she went out with her sisters, she had no qualms about eating bacon and ham. She even enjoyed a good lobster once in a while.

Mom's half-sisters, Phyllis, Eva, and Ceil meant everything to her. All of her sisters lived into their 80s. Their husbands and children frequently visited the Lesser Lodge. Mom also had two half-brothers, Benjamin and William, of whom she was also very fond.

My mother was a good business woman. As a child she had diphtheria and had part of her vocal cords removed, and this had given her a gruff voice that she used to advantage. When she wanted something constructed, for instance, it was constructed—and just the way she wanted. My mother had no reticence in telling the carpenters exactly what she wanted done.

Back row standing left to right: William Margolies (Mom's brother), Phyllis Margolies Mantel (Mom's sister), Ben Stern (Mom's brother-in-law), Ben Margolies (Mom's brother). Bottom row: Lillian Margolies (Mom's sister-in-law), Mike Silverstein and Sophie Silverstein (friends), Ceil Margolies Stern (Mom's sister), and Gussie Margolies (Mom's sister-in-law).

My mother made the decisions concerning new construction but permitted my father to worry about the payments that resulted. When there was no construction being done during the winter and Mom was in the city, she did the cooking. To make sure the family was healthy, Mom fried all the meats, including steak. At times, Mom made matzoh ball soup. No one needed to worry about stomach cramps. The matzoh balls dropped directly down to your feet. Had David used one of my mom's matzoh balls when he slew Goliath, it would have been just as lethal.

My mother used to make something they called "shmudder case" for the eating pleasure of her sisters and herself. The word, *case*, in Yiddish means cheese. Mom used to take some kind of cheese, wrap it in cloth, and place it on the ledge outside the window of our tenement house. After a while, the cheese stank to high heaven. Even the rag men who came into the courtyard shouting, "I cash cloths," stood as far as they could get from the *shmudder case*. When her sisters came in the house, they all ate the cheese. The Bush administration wouldn't have needed to torture people by water boarding if they'd forced them to eat shmudder case— they would have gotten more confessions but it would have been less humane. Incidentally, the father of the Jewish actor Kirk Douglas was in the "I cash cloths" business.

When I did something wrong, Mom wacked me pretty good, but always with love. Even though she was the disciplinarian in the household, I was not afraid of her. It was my father I feared. He never hit me, but when he glared at me I was terrified.

Once, in the dead of winter, the ground piled high with snow, my mother was drying me off after a bath. My brother told my mother about something bad I had done. My mother came at me, but I ran for the door and continued running, bare-ass naked over the snow with my mother in close pursuit. Finally, after we had run quite some distance, my mom gave up the chase. My mother was such a loving and wonderful person that if she had caught me she probably would have hugged me and kissed me, and as she held me in her arms she would have burst out into laughter at the ridiculousness of the situation.

Me and Mom (circa 1944)

When my mother went to sleep, she had no need of a sleeping pill. She kept a bottle of scotch by the side of the bed and, when she was unable to sleep, Mom took a shot directly from the bottle. She never ever drank during the day. During the day, my mom always had a cup of coffee in her hand. When the chauffeur drove her to town, she had a cup of coffee clutched in her hand. When she was in the office, she had coffee by her side. It is strange but true; when others went to the safe, they sometimes found a cup of coffee inside.

Mom was an avid antique hunter. She took the back roads to see farmers and asked if they had antiques they wished to sell. She bought many antiques, some of which I still have.

Mom worked extremely hard during the summer season. She oversaw everything and frequently had to walk uphill from the first level to the second. It was a terrible strain on her. There were no golf carts in those days for her to use.

She also worked hard during the off-season when the building improvements took place, having to advise the carpenters and other workmen as to exactly what she wanted. In addition, Mom did the cooking. All of this was extremely difficult for a person who had high blood pressure. Mom passed away in 1957 at the age of 62. High blood pressure and hard work took its toll.

My parents went to visit Cuba in 1937. They went with my wife Evelyn's parents. Since this was well before Castro seized power, they were able to go to restaurants, see shows, and gamble. Aside from visits to Florida, this was the only vacation they ever took.

One year they purchased a home on an island in Florida in partnership with the owners of the Jefferson Steam Laundry, who did the washing of the hotel's laundry. After a couple of years, they sold the home at a profit, but not nearly as large a one had they sold it a few years later.

GLORIA KATZ (1924)

My cousin, Gloria Katz, tells the story of how she and a friend named Marilyn Broder went to the Lesser Lodge and slept in the same double bed. Gloria's parents slept in the other double bed. Upon checking out, Gloria received a bill for $5 per night and her friend Marilyn received a bill for $3 per night. Gloria questioned my mom as to why she was paying more than her friend considering they had both arrived on the same date and both had shared a bed. My mom told her, "you were the third person in the room and your friend was the fourth."

Gloria Katz

Gloria also tells the story of "when I was about six, I was forced to share a bed with an old lady. I woke up in the middle of the night due to being bitten by her teeth. They were not in her mouth."

IT'S A "HOTEL" (1923)

A "hotel" in the Catskills is a place where a guest is provided not only a room, but also food and entertainment free of additional charge. By comparison, in a "rooming house" only the room is provided. Guests there must purchase and cook their own meals and few additional amenities are provided.

MAIN HOUSE (1923)

The lower floor of the main house consisted of a kitchen, an adjoining bedroom, and a living room area.

On the second floor were four bedrooms and a bathroom. The front of the house had a wide porch.

When I attended the Midway School, I slept in one of the bedrooms on the second floor. In the corner of the room there was a 20-inch-square hole covered by a grate. This aperture was supposed to permit the heat from the lobby, which was directly below the room, to flow upward and warm my room. It was great theoretically but it did not work in actuality. The theory of hot air rising through a grate is just that—hot air.

I used to sleep on two mattresses with an eight-inch feather tick covering me. Incidentally, my father, who never struck me in my entire life, decided to punish me for some bit of mischief I had supposedly perpetrated. I was probably innocent, but Dad punished me nevertheless. He took off his belt and struck several vicious blows on my eight-inch feather tick. Naturally, I couldn't feel a thing. But he was satisfied he had done his duty as a father and I was satisfied because the punishment had been completely painless.

In 1928, my father was driving his old jalopy when he had an accident. There were five passengers in the auto including me. The car rolled over three times but, amazingly, no one was injured. That was the next-to-the-last-time my dad drove a car.

The very last time was twelve years later. I was teaching my mom how to drive, and it being 1940, that included learning the delicate skill of operating the clutch while shifting the gears. The lesson I was teaching at the time was how to shift into reverse, and I explained to Mom how to step on the clutch, shift into gear, and then release the clutch slowly to put the car in motion. Over and over I explained, but Mom couldn't quite get the hang of it. Finally my father got disgusted and said, "Let me show you how to do it." He got into the driver's seat, stepped on the clutch, put the car in reverse, released the clutch, and the vehicle zoomed backwards. Upon hearing me scream "brake, brake, brake," he slammed on the brakes and the car screeched to a stop, stalling the engine. He never drove a car again.

BUNGALOW (1923)

When the property was purchased, there was an old bungalow a short distance from the main house. It was an ugly building, a real eyesore. As it got older, it got even uglier. My brother and sister and I begged our parents to replace it with something nicer, but to no avail; it remained where it was, a true monument to ugliness.

In it were two small bathrooms each containing a commode but no shower or bathtub. Each of the eight rooms had a sink. The rooms in the bungalow were, as you would expect, the least expensive to rent. They were rented, but only to a select group—those who did not shower or bathe.

WHITE SULPHUR SPRINGS (1923)

White Sulphur Springs was so named because of the springs in the area. These were popular in the late 1800s because of the heath-giving properties people thought were contained in the sulphur. By the 1920s, few active springs remained.

The town of White Sulphur Springs is located between Liberty and the Lesser Lodge. When the lodge's chauffeurs needed gasoline for their gas-guzzling cars, they went to the White Sulphur Springs gas station. Gasoline cost eight cents a gallon. A car could be filled for about $1.50.

Martin Hanofee's Garage – White Sulphur Springs (1923).
The Happiness House faces forward at far end of street.

John Joyner was the postmaster and the owner of the building that housed the post office servicing the community. The building was divided into two parts. The post office half was located in one part and contained boxes for the mail recipients to pick up their mail. There was no mail delivery; the mail had to be picked up at the post office. It had a teller's window for those who wished to purchase stamps, send money orders, and pick up packages.

The other half of the building was a grocery store where the local people could do their shopping. Sometimes, when the hotel needed items in a hurry, the chauffeur would be dispatched to "Joyner's" to pick up the needed items.

As mentioned earlier, I had no birth certificate. When it came time for me to register for the draft I found it necessary to prove to the army I was old enough to get killed. John Joyner was one of the three people who attested to my age.

John Joyner's store had a competitor named the Fishbeins who also sold groceries. Their store was on the ground floor and the Fishbeins lived on the second floor. Mr. and Mrs. Fishbein had three sons. When my parents had to be out of town for several days, they left me with the Fishbeins. Their sons were strong as an ox and we used to have friendly royal battles.

In White Sulphur Springs there was a medium-sized hotel named the Hotel Leona, owned by a Mr. Sobel. The Leona was the first hotel in White Sulphur Springs to have a swimming pool. Considering there were only two swimming pools in all of White Sulphur Springs, this was quite an accomplishment.

There was one other hotel in White Sulphur Springs. It was originally named Happiness House. This was a small hotel. Its name was later changed to

"Hotel Tel Aviv." I suppose the hotel felt too many gentiles were coming as guests.

White Sulphur Springs also had a small synagogue. It seated about seventy people and was never crowded, except on the holidays, but some Jews used to go there religiously. My parents did not frequent the synagogue. My father had religiously studied all aspects of Hebrew in Poland and was qualified to be a rabbi. As necessary, he conducted religious services at the hotel.

Also located in White Sulphur Springs was a bar and grill named Hanofees. Many nights, after the show, some guests and I—and whichever girl I happened to be going with at the time—went to the bar. It was owned by a widow and she had two sons; one was called Stretch. I never found out his true name, but as you can imagine, he was very tall. Stretch worked for Grossinger's Hotel. His younger brother Gene went to law school and became a judge. In addition to the beer, we'd go there for entertainment.

The two brothers would sing and I can recall them singing "It's the same old shillelagh my father brought from Ireland." Years later I found out a *shillelagh* was a "cudgel." And later still, I found out a *cudgel* was a "cane." I learned two words by drinking beer. Perhaps if I drank something stronger, like whiskey, I would have a tremendous vocabulary.

My brother Seymour was very friendly with a young man named Lenny Rosen who lived with his father in White Sulphur Springs. They both were five years older than I. Very infrequently would they permit me to be in their company. One day I was invited by Lenny to visit their home. When I got there I found a veritable treasure trove of turn-of-the-century newspaper comics. My favorite was the Katzenjammer Kids. I think I must be one of the few people living today who remembers the Katzenjammer Kids.[12]

Lenny and my brother formed an egg-selling partnership. They purchased a car, bought eggs wholesale, and sold them door-to-door. At times, even though I was only nine years old, I went door-to-door to sell eggs for them. Their egg business did not last long and after they went out of business, Lenny took the car that belonged to the partnership.

My father was incensed because he felt that Lenny had absconded with the auto, half of which belonged to my brother. He collected my mother, my brother, and me, and we all boarded the BMT, the Brooklyn Manhattan Transit. We went a few stops and eventually accosted Lenny and a friend of his.

In no time at all a fist fight broke out. I found myself being dragged by my heels. Fortunately, however, my father got a few blows in. That was the last time I saw either Lenny or my brother's half of the car.

Today, White Sulphur Springs is a full-grown town with many beautiful homes, businesses, and restaurants.

KATZ'S BAKERY

The hotel bought the rye bread it needed from Katz's Bakery. Katz's Bakery was located on a hill above Liberty that had intersecting roads that offered easy access to Swan Lake, White Sulphur Springs, and Liberty. They made real rye and pumpernickel bread. The bottom of their bread was white and hard, the crust was also hard, and the inside was wonderful. It was real Jewish rye and I am unable to find its equal in any bakery today.

The Lesser Lodge ordered all its bread from Katz's and it was always delivered on time. In those days, dough not only went farther, it went faster.

Katz's Bakery later bought an outlet for its bread in Liberty. In addition to bread, they sold all types of cookies and cakes. The bakery also had stores in Monticello and was to become a "destination" for many a resident, especially the summer residents who flocked to the Catskills to escape the city heat. Katz's remained in business until 1989. The building was acquired by the Liberty Chamber of Commerce in 1995 for a museum and arts center.[13]

OFFICE (1923)

In the early years of the 1900s, the telephone system operated completely different than it does today. Seven to ten people would have the same telephone number. This was called a "party line." When that number was called, the operator would ask to whom the caller wished to speak—no one was able to dial anyone directly.

Our telephone number was "1060R." There were seven people on our party line. Each of us had a different ring. If the operator rang two short rings and one long ring, it meant the call was for us.

Everyone on a party line was able to listen to the conversations regardless of who was called. If you wanted to hear the local gossip, all you need do was to gently pick up the receiver when the telephone was in use.

Later on, a telephone call could be made directly to the hotel. The hotel telephone operator plugged a line into a switchboard connecting the incoming call to the room of the person being phoned.

All telephone calls had to be made using the service of the hotel telephone operator.

Sometimes the guests gave their cash to the office for safekeeping. Occasionally the hotel would need to send checks to creditors without having sufficient funds in the bank to cover the checks issued. We used the funds left by the guests for safekeeping. When we took the cash, we'd replace it with a slip of paper enumerating the amount of cash taken to the bank. Any shortage was resolved on Sundays when the guests paid their bills.

Ruth Caplan worked as a bookkeeper in the office for many years until she passed away. Ruth advised my future wife, Evelyn, not to marry me. Evelyn and I were dating on a steady basis. Ruth was Evelyn's aunt. She told Evelyn she had known me for a few years and I would not be faithful. But despite this wise advice, Evelyn married me and I turned out to be a wonderful husband, although perhaps a bit too modest. Ruth was to become our son's Godmother.

TRAVELING FROM NEW YORK CITY (1923)

The guests who came to the Lesser Lodge from New York City traveled by car, bus, or train. Traveling by car, the most commonly used mode of transportation, wasn't easy during those years. Frequently, autos overheated and spewed steam from the radiator. Then the people would have to wait until the radiator cooled so they could add water.

Cars were not as powerful then as they are today. Going uphill in the Wurtsboro Mountains was difficult. The reverse gear in autos was more powerful than the forward gear and many cars were forced to drive in reverse to climb the mountains. The Wurtsboro Mountains are over 10 miles long and extremely steep.

Back then, no driver ever received a ticket for speeding while ascending the Wurtsboro Mountains.

BOWERY (1924)

When businesses, rooming houses, and hotels in the Catskills needed handymen, they would sometimes call one of several employment agencies that used limousines to pick up drunkards in "The Bowery," an area in lower Manhattan known for its drunkards, squalor, and filth.

The handymen—for whom the employment agency charged $5.00 for each delivered—were generally good people but prone to alcoholism. Many could remain sober for only a relatively short period of time. They were Americans and Europeans. These handymen were paid $20 a month plus room and board.

The term *handyman* is generic. A handyman could be someone who cleaned, someone who washed the dishes, or someone who painted, and so on. A handyman could also be a female, who would serve, for example as a chambermaid.

There were occasions when, after we had paid the $5.00 agency fee, a handyman would skip out, not even doing one day's work. I guess he felt hopping a limousine was an inexpensive way of going from one place to another.

HANDYMEN—FIRST MEMORIES (1924)

During the summers and winters we stayed in the Catskills, from 1923 to 1932, handymen were hired by the hotel to make minor improvements, do manual labor, and to paint. I recall when I was five or six years old, they were busy, among other things, spackling the eight-room bungalow—applying plaster-like material to the walls of the room and then using a trowel to make designs.

One of my first memories was that of the handymen conversing in the kitchen, joking and singing songs like:

Where do you worka John,

In the Dela Lok a Wan,[14]

Where do you worka Marie

In the telephone company

When the day's work was done, the family and the handymen would all have dinner in the kitchen. The daily fare usually consisted of soup, bread, coffee, potatoes, and large tomato herrings. At times we would have chicken or some other inexpensive item instead of the herring. We would then sit around listening to the radio or conversing. Oh, how well I remember "The Shadow," "Little Orphan Annie," and the "Little Theater on Times Square." And how about Mayor LaGuardia reading the funnies every Sunday?

1ST AND 2ND COOKS (1924)

Over the years we had various 1st cooks. Cooks usually worked at the hotel for four or five years but only during the summer season. In the earlier years, 1st cooks were paid $200 a week. In the later years, they received $300 a week. A good 1st cook was very important. After all, when the food served at a hotel is not good, the guests will not come back the next season.

The 2nd cook's job was to prepare the dairy meals and assist the 1st cook in any way he could. The 2nd cooks were paid half as much as the 1st cook.

Sometimes my brother and I would help out. Many times, when the 2nd cook had too much to do, my brother (or sometimes both of us) would cook breakfast.

At times the dish washers became drunk. When they did, I had to wash the dishes. Washing the dishes took me a long time because when I washed the dishes they actually came out clean. Luckily, my washing of dishes ended when a dishwashing machine was installed.

The last 1st cook of the hotel was named Sam Zemicov. He was assisted by his wife. The 2nd cook was named Battle—and he was a big man. No one battled with Battle.

Hotels the size of ours needed only one 1st cook, who primarily cooked the meat meals. He used large ovens that cooked the various foods. The hotel also had a large grill, custom made for us, which was capable of grilling 25 steaks at a time. Steaks made on a grill are always better tasting than steaks made using an oven.

When serving food to the guests, the waiters lined up in front of the cook in order to receive the food. The cook had three stacks of fifteen dishes in front of him. The dishes had been kept in special heated compartments in order to keep them warm.

The 1st cook, his wife, and the 2nd cook would work as a team to dole out the food. For example, one cook placed the meat on the plate, one of the other two placed the vegetables and the third the potatoes. The waiters would then take the food and stack the dishes on his or her tray, usually ten plates per tray. This type of serving arrangement is called a "station." The food was hot, as was the kitchen.

Some foods, like French fries, were best dished out by hand. Then the servers would dip their fingers in ice water every now and then for relief.

When the hotel had many guests we had a double station. That is, there would be six people dishing out the food, and the food came out of the kitchen twice as fast.

THE DINING ROOM AND GUEST QUARTERS (1927)

My parents realized that although they had done decently with the few rooms they had, they could make a better living by adding rooms and further improving the hotel.

In 1927, a dining room was added and eight rooms were built above the dining room. As a result, the total number of bedrooms on the second floor was increased to 12. In addition, the partitions between the old kitchen, bedroom, and lobby were eliminated, thereby creating a spacious lobby—about 45 by 45 feet.

The eight bedrooms above the kitchen were extremely small and had been added to the four small bedrooms acquired in 1923. As I said, the rooms were extremely small. To make matters worse, the guests in all twelve rooms shared the one bathroom that existed at the time the original house had been acquired. But the fact the bathroom contained a bath and shower permitted us to advertise them as deluxe accommodations. Well, it wasn't an outhouse.

A photograph of the main building as it existed before 1934 is shown below, just before the entire front façade was changed to incorporate the porch area into the dining room and lobby.

MAIN HOUSE, THE LESSER LODGE, WHITE SULPHUR SPRINGS, N.-Y.

Lesser Lodge Main Building Postcard (1927)

MATERIALS AND SUPPLIES (1927)

Lumber for all the buildings was furnished by the Kohler family located in Jeffersonville. The plumbing fixtures were purchased in Jeffersonville from another company. General supplies were purchased from Sabloff's in Liberty. These purchases were generally made on credit. The obligation for these purchases would be paid off during the season, provided there was money available. If the hotel was unable to pay the total amount owed, the creditors would defer the unpaid obligation and permit the hotel to pay the balance the following season.

The owners of these businesses knew my parents were honorable people who would pay as soon as they could.

The name "Jeffersonville" came from the village's first hotel, the Jefferson House, named in honor of U.S. President Thomas Jefferson.

PLUMBERS (1927)

The plumbers who worked for the hotel would, for some perverse reason, sometimes install the hot water tap on the left side where it belonged, but on others they would install it on the right. This would result in many calls to the office complaining of a lack of hot water.

To ease the problem of mismatched faucets, the plumbers installed a circulator in the cellar of the main house. A circulator is a device that keeps hot water flowing through the pipes 24 hours a day. As each cycle is completed, the water is reheated in the burner and the circulator once again pumps the hot water through the hot water pipes. This enables a user to have hot water immediately when they turn on the faucet. I suppose the plumbers found this easier than connecting the hot water line to the left tap and the cold water line to the right tap. That being said, many of the taps were mismarked anyway, so some guests still had to guess where the hot water would be. The circulator made things easier by enabling the guests to more quickly guess correctly and this resulted in fewer calls to the office.

When the lobby was being renovated, it was discovered that the floor of the lobby directly over the old cellar was sagging. There was a possibility of the lobby falling into the cellar! Since it would have been very expensive to construct wooden supports to level the lobby floor, the carpenters merely installed four ten-foot jacks similar to the jack for a car, and the problem was solved. They simply jacked up the lobby floor until it was level.

Before the new cellar and kitchen were constructed, a bad odor had pervaded the old lobby and the main house. After several days, I discovered why. I went into the old cellar from where the foundation and subsurface of the main house could be seen, and observed that the connection to the sewer system had broken. As matter was flushed down the toilets, it had been going beneath the main house instead of through the drain pipes.

Once the cause of the odor was discovered, the plumbers quickly fixed the connection, the subsurface was cleaned, and the sweet smell of Catskill Mountain air once again filled the main house.

PURCHASE AGREEMENT

The purchase agreement enumerated that my parents acquired a heavy sleigh, a bay horse, five cows, and 250 chickens.

Since neither of my parents were good at driving an automobile, having the sleigh and bay horse was a boon. My parents used them to go shopping in town. After they made their purchases, we would return home accompanied by the pleasant tinkle of bells. Every time we went shopping, it seemed like Christmas.

The five cows were another matter. In the winter, we provided them with hay. In the warm months, they grazed. But no matter whether they ate hay or grass, the amount of manure they produced was prodigious. The cows also had to be milked. We enjoyed the milk they produced, but city slickers are not renowned for their ability to withdraw the milk from a cow. We decided it was easier to buy milk than to clean up the manure and milk the cows, and the cows were sold.

The barn provided shelter for the animals and poultry. It contained a hayloft in which the chickens lived and laid their eggs. Lots of them! I liked raw eggs and would make a small hole on both ends of the shell and suck the egg out. One day I consumed a dozen eggs. After I became ill, my love for eggs diminished in direct proportion to the nausea they induced.

The barn had been built on a stone foundation, and between the bottom of the barn and the ground was a space approximately three feet in height. In this area lived a family of skunks that apparently fed on poultry and eggs. The skunks had not been mentioned in the purchase agreement sale.

Part of the stone foundation had been taken out so that one could peer under the barn. We had a neighbor named Mr. Kratz who lived a quarter of a mile east of the hotel on Route 52 toward White Sulphur Springs. Occasionally, Mr. Kratz would come to the gap in the foundation of the barn armed with a powerful flashlight and a shotgun. He would shine the flashlight on a skunk—which would stand as if mesmerized—and shoot it. The shotgun pellets spread out over a four-foot area, so even if the shotgun was poorly aimed, it would instantly kill the skunk before it could emit its terrible odor. Eventually, thanks to Mr. Kratz, the barn was completely "deskunked."

Mr. Kratz was a man of German descent and to me he looked old. I was a kid and anyone over 20 looked old. We were very fond of Mr. Kratz. He would also show us tricks. He would make a needle float in water. He would fill a saucer with water, place a lighted piece of paper in an inverted cup, turn it over, and after a short interval, the cup would soak up the water. We were amazed.

THE BATTLE OF BUNKER HILL

When I was about five years old in 1927, my parents decided to convert the barn into additional rooms. The exterior of the barn was unchanged but the entire interior was dismantled and a floor was built. Partitions were then constructed so that the inside contained five large rooms and one small room. The Lesser Lodge, "For all the Best in FUN and REST," was taking shape.[15]

The barn had been constructed with a tin roof. When it rained, the pounding of the rain made it sound like the Battle of Bunker Hill was still in progress. Even though it was loud and noisy, I took pleasure in the sound. Many years later, when I was in the army and had to sleep in a tent from time to time, the sound of rain beating on the tent was pleasurable to me. Likely it brought back some memories of my youth.

The small room in what had been the barn was used by my grandfather Jacob. He spent the summer gratis. My grandfather was very good to me. He bought cherries and other goodies for me. An ice cream truck would come by every day and I would ask, "Grandpa, can I have a nickel for ice cream?" He would always interrupt his pinochle game and give me a nickel.

Grandpa enjoyed eating small fish. He bought a small metal fishing trap. The fishing trap was oval with large round holes at both ends each leading to a passage that narrowed toward the center of the trap. Grandpa baited the trap with bread. The fish would enter the trap through one of the large holes, swim up the passage toward the bait, but were unable to escape because they were not clever enough to know they could exit the trap through the small holes.

LONESOME (1925)

Until 1931, when I was nine years old, I spent every winter at the Lesser Lodge. Later, we would only winter in the hotel if construction was planned. When I was an infant, it didn't bother me, but as I got older and began to understand, I realized something was wrong. I was lonely, but I was at that age unable to define it.

I recall when I was about four years old being left outdoors, in my carriage, with nobody attending me. It started to rain and the harder the rain fell, the harder I cried. I don't remember how the incident ended, but I distinctly remember the rain falling and my discomfort.

During the season, we had guests who brought their children and with their presence, that feeling left me. Gradually, I began to understand that what I was experiencing was loneliness.

Because I was so lonely during the winter, I asked guests to speak to my father and ask him if we, the family, "were going to the City." The City was my generic name for the Bronx, Brooklyn, or any area that had children.

Even when I attended Midway School, I had no relief from loneliness. Being the only Jew in school seemed to set up a barrier. No one made any effort to be my friend.

The only winter this dreaded loneliness seemed to lessen was the year my cousin, Bernie Rader, and his mother wintered at the hotel. Even though he was a year and a half younger than I, I had someone to play with. I don't remember the circumstances that permitted him to spend the winter with us. I asked Bernie but he, too, doesn't remember.

It would be another three years before I had my first real friend, "Took." Once we met, we became nearly inseparable.

BURNING CROSSES (1923)

As previously mentioned, the hotel had rooms on various levels. On one occasion the guests on the highest level looked out to see a fearsome sight—a large burning cross. The guests were very perturbed. This had never happened before. Who had done it? It might have been the Klu Klux Klan or perhaps just some mischievous kids. We never found out. But we were glad that it never happened again.

SAM HELLER (1928)

Youngsville was another Sleepy Hollow-type town. It was located about a mile and a half to the West of the hotel. It contained Sam Heller's store, a few other stores, and an automobile repair shop. To the West of the town there were two moderately-sized hotels.

When I was six years old, I had a stupid habit of throwing pebbles at cars as they passed on Route 52. One day I made the mistake of throwing pebbles at Sam Heller's Truck. He stopped and chased me. He caught me and delivered a few well-deserved slaps to my behind and told me if I ever did it again he would make the slaps much harder and also tell my parents. That broke the habit. I never again threw pebbles at a car.

THE MIDWAY SCHOOL (1928)

I was a student at the Midway School for four years beginning in 1928 (ages six through nine). Midway School was so named because it was located midway between Youngsville to the West and White Sulphur Springs to the East. At that time, Midway Road started at Route 52 and ran perpendicular to it.

The school was conveniently located 250 yards to the West of the main house of the Lesser Lodge and I was able to walk to the school.[16] The school had a maximum capacity of about forty students. It was about 60 in length and 50 feet in width. The school was entered from the side and had two anterooms about eight feet wide, one for boys and one for girls. The walls contained hooks to hang coats and other items. The bathrooms were located in this area. In the back of the classroom was a large heating device which supplied enough heat so that the room was relatively warm.

Midway School was very different from the schools of today. It had just one teacher who taught all the grades. This is how it was done. The teacher had a desk in the front of the room. Directly in front of this desk there were two backed benches capable of seating eight children. The teacher would call out "first grade" and the children in the first grade would leave their own desks and sit on the benches in front of the teacher's desk. The teacher would then instruct those children on the bench, asking them questions and assigning them homework.

The Lesser Lodge was located between Midway Road and Lesser Lake (shown to the right).

Sometimes, when the students he was teaching didn't know an answer, he would call the name of another student in a different grade and ask that student for the answer. He would frequently call on me. I generally knew the answer.

While the children in the various grades, each in turn, sat on the bench in front of the teacher, all the other students in the classroom were permitted to either listen to the teacher or study. On other occasions, when the teacher was discussing a matter of interest to all, such as writing or current events, there were no students on the benches. Then everyone would be expected to listen from their own desks and participate in the lesson.

In or around 1959, the school building was auctioned by the county. My parents bid at the auction but they were outbid and the building was purchased by a couple with children. Later on I think my parents were sorry they had not bid more.

Contrary to reports, the Midway School building was *never* used by either hotel (Lesser Lodge or Kramer's Union House) as staff housing or otherwise.[17]

It had simply lain dormant and unkempt for many years before it was auctioned.

Discipline

When a student behaved badly, the teacher would tell that individual to report to one of the anterooms, where the student would be the recipient of a solid spanking. The teacher, Stanley Steele, was a strong man and the spanking he administered was solid enough to ensure good behavior.

In the class, there was a developmentally disabled, well-developed young lady who frequently misbehaved. The teacher would spank her when she misbehaved. I don't know who enjoyed the spanking more—the teacher or the young lady. Perhaps that is why she misbehaved.

Jew (1928)

At the beginning of each day, the teacher recited the Lord's Prayer. I got to know it pretty well but I didn't think it applied to me. With my scant knowledge of religion, I didn't know whether it came from the New or Old Testament. I didn't know whether the Lord's Prayer was universal or only applied to gentiles.

I was the only Jew in the school. My fellow students didn't display any obvious anti-Semitism, but I did sense an undercurrent. The only time I sensed a greater degree of anti-Semitism was when some of the other students arranged for me to fight another student named Kenneth. He was as eager to fight as I was, but all we did was dance around each other.

I didn't know the first thing about politics but, in retrospect, I think they and their families must have

43

been Republicans. I heard the chant many times, "dried rats, pickled rats, all for the Democrats!"

Took (1928)

My first and, at the time, only real friend was named Took. His real name was Harold Tremper. He lived in his grandfather's farmhouse located on a hill on the south side of Route 52. He and I were inseparable. We were pals from the first day of school. We used to walk along Route 52 looking for cigarette butts that people driving autos had thrown out the window. Long cigarette butts were a prized possession.

On Took's farm there was a large rock formation left over from the Ice Age. We used to sit on top of the rock formation, feet dangling, smoking the butts. After smoking butts for some time Took got his hands on some chewing tobacco. We both indulged. We both got sick and swore off chewing tobacco for life.

FISHING & HUNTING

Took and I fished with our hands. That is, we would watch the fish and when they swam into a hole in the water bank, we would reach into the hole with our bare hands and grab the fish. At night our parents would clean and cook them.

On one of our fishing excursions, we saw a snake about 25 inches long. It had a half swallowed fish in its mouth. The snake was able to evade us although it was hindered by the fish in its mouth.

Took and I thought it was great sport killing snakes by snapping them. We would take the snake by the tail and snap it, thereby breaking its spine. One day, I had spotted a snake with its tail under some debris. To get to the tail I pulled the middle of the snake toward me, and the snake bit me. Luckily, the snakes in that area were not poisonous. But after that experience, our killing of snakes ceased.

Took and I also fished with a rod, a length of string, and a hook. But there was one type of fish we could not hook. They are called suckers. They always stayed on the bottom, unmoving, and would not bite the delicious food we offered, so we were unable to hook them. The aforementioned Mr. Kratz solved the problem. He told us to take about six inches of thin wire, attach one end to our rod and make a noose with the other end. We gently slipped the noose under and over the fish and jerked hard. We were then able to enjoy the taste of sucker at dinnertime.

FOUL WATERS (1928)

My father had masons install a large water-holding tank constructed of cement on top of the high hill. The tank was located considerably higher than the top of the houses we had built. Its purpose was to ensure the hotel would have plenty of water in all the houses at all times. Because the water was stored at a much higher level than the hotel, gravity would provide the pressure needed. When the holding tank got low, water was automatically pumped from the well. The well was deep and the water was very cold.

Took and I decided we would breed fish; we took a dozen of the fish we had caught by hand and put them in the holding tank. Within a few days, out of their environment, the fish died. Needless to say, this caused quite a bit of consternation. The water stank of dead fish. The guests complained.

We had to bury the fish, the holding tank had to be drained, the walls had to be cleaned and fresh water pumped into the holding tank. But more importantly, my parents had to be mollified, which was not easy. My mother gave me a good beating.

My mother believed in the old adage, "spare the rod and spoil the child." She wasn't cruel, but she was 100 percent right. She taught me to respect teachers, police, and my elders, something for which I, in time, came to thank her. And besides, she never really hurt me.

THE MIDWAY HILL

When I was about ten years old, my Aunt Sadie bought a sled for me. My brother Seymour and I went sledding down the steep Midway Road. I was on the bottom holding onto the sled. My brother was stretched out over me and holding on to me. About three quarters of the way down, sledding at a good speed, we hit a patch of sand. The sled and I came to a grinding halt but my brother flew down the rest of the hill, across Route 52, and into a snow bank. He was so impacted in the snow bank that I had to pull him out by his feet.

IMPROVEMENTS IN GENERAL

With the passage of time, many improvements and renovations were made to the hotel. New housing for guests was erected, a casino was built, and a tennis court, a large swimming pool, a lake, four handball courts, a baseball field, and a day camp for children were all added one by one.

At its demise, in 1963, the hotel could accommodate 250 adults and a large number of children.

THE DEPRESSION YEARS (1929)

During the years of the Great Depression, when air conditioning had not yet been invented and there was a limited amount of air travel, people in the cities sweltered. They went to sleep half-naked with the fans on. Others slept on their fire escapes in order to get some measure of relief. The one escape available to many city dwellers during the hot summer was going to the Catskills, where the weather was much cooler and dryer.

Only people who had jobs were in a financial position to come to the Lesser Lodge. Many others were finding it difficult just to purchase bread. The lyrics of the song "Brother, Can You Spare a Dime" describe how bad things were during the Great Depression.

Brother, Can You Spare a Dime[18]

They used to tell me I was building a dream, and so I followed the mob,
When there was earth to plow, or guns to bear, I was always there right on the job.
They used to tell me I was building a dream, with peace and glory ahead,
Why should I be standing in line, just waiting for bread?
Once I built a railroad, I made it run, made it race against time.
Once I built a railroad; now it's done. Brother, can you spare a dime?
Once I built a tower, up to the sun, brick, and rivet, and lime;
Once I built a tower, now it's done. Brother, can you spare a dime?

> *Once in khaki suits, gee we looked swell,*
> *Full of that Yankee Doodly Dum,*
> *Half a million boots went slogging through Hell,*
> *And I was the kid with the drum!*

Say, don't you remember, they called me Al; it was Al all the time.
Why don't you remember, I'm your pal? Buddy, can you spare a dime?

> *Once in khaki suits, gee we looked swell,*
> *Full of that Yankee Doodly Dum,*
> *Half a million boots went slogging through Hell,*
> *And I was the kid with the drum!*

Say, don't you remember, they called me Al; it was Al all the time.
Say, don't you remember, I'm your pal? Buddy, can you spare a dime?

ENTERTAINMENT IN THE DINING ROOM (1927-1933)

To provide entertainment for the guests, the dining room was used. The tables in the dining room were cleared and a record player was set up to provide music for dancing. Later in the evening, chairs would be lined up for a show.

The shows were put on by the staff and they were often about unions and the advantages they provided the workers. At times, the staff and guests performed. Sometimes the children performed in the shows. I recall my sister and I doing Hansel and Gretel. At times, even though there was no band, staff or guests would provide entertainment by singing. It was a period when the small things in life were sought after for simple pleasure. Times were very bad; a band would be an unaffordable luxury.

Stories about the old country were frequently told in the dining room. They were told in Yiddish and they covered the period from the late 18th century to the early 19th century. Here's an example, originally spoken in Yiddish:

The Rabbi and the Rebitzen (the Rabbi's wife) officiated in a one-room synagogue which had one glass window. Their problem, on a prayer day, was they had only nine men for minion and needed ten, one more. (In Jewish law there must be ten people present when services are being conducted.) The Rebitzen was old, ugly, and fat and had a shawl over her head. Finally she spied a man crossing the street and rushed out to meet him.

Breathlessly she said to him, "Do you want to be the tenth?"

He replied, "Do I want to be the tenth? No! Not even the first."

Here's another—

The marriage arranger in this little town in Poland says to Becky, "Becky, have I got a perfect marriage for you; don't ask, it's the Count—he is wealthy and has a beautiful home. He can give you a magnificent carriage with two horses; he can give you anything you could possibly want." Becky replies, "I can't marry the Count because he is only half Jewish." The arranger says, "But Becky, you are hunched-backed, have one leg shorter than the other, you are cock-eyed, not good looking, and missing a few teeth." Becky finally agrees to marry the Count. The marriage arranger then says, "Magnificent, great, now I'll go and ask the Count if he wants to marry you."

SINGER'S RESTAURANT (1930-1963)

Singer's Restaurant, located in Liberty, was like the Town Meeting Hall. All the entertainers and the late-nighters met at Singer's. Singer's served all the popular goodies: corned beef, pastrami, tongue, and so on.

After the show and dancing, my date and I would often go to Singer's. We met many entertainers there. The comedians were almost invariably Jewish, the dancers were almost invariably gentile, and the singers were mixed. During and after a meal, the comedians would mix with the audience and tell stories and jokes. I knew most of the entertainers because they performed at our hotel.

SABLOFF'S (1923-1963)

Sabloff's, also located in Liberty, supplied all the hotels within the area with paint and hardware. They also handled many other supplies a hotel needed. Practically every day our car went to Sabloff's to buy supplies. When construction was taking place, they furnished most of the necessary materials.

One morning my dad went to Sabloff's to purchase ten gallons of grey paint. They said they did not have grey paint in stock. My father asked how soon he would be able to get it. They said in 20 minutes. Dad asked how that was possible. They said, simple: we'll mix five gallons of black paint with five gallons of white paint and it will be ready in 20 minutes.

Lobby Ventilation Disaster (1930)

In the hotel's lobby, there was a metal grating and a furnace below, which supplied the lobby with a moderate amount of heat during cold weather. Although the heat supplied was inadequate, the situation was not improved when the son of one of the guests urinated through the grating. The aroma lingered for weeks. That same child, the very same day, removed the caps from three dozen Coca Cola bottles. Fortunately, the following year the guest sent his son to sleep-away camp. Better the son create havoc there.

Heat (1930)

In my room on the first floor, there was an 18-inch square opening made in the floor that, theoretically, would permit the heat from the furnace under the lobby to rise and heat the room in which I slept. I had two mattresses and a huge feather tick on my bed, but it was still cold. I told my parents what I really needed was a furnace in my room.

I lived at the hotel summer and winter until I was about 10 years old. The summers were wonderful but the winters were bitterly cold. When I say bitterly cold I mean *bitterly* cold. All construction was done during the "off season," a more pleasant way of saying October through May.

When building was being done, "salamanders" were used to provide heat. A salamander is a portable stove which supplies a great deal of heat. Winters in the Catskills were so cold that when you faced a salamander, the front of your body was fine, but the back of your body was still cold.

MRS. LAWLESS (1930)

Mrs. Lawless was a widow who owned a considerable amount of land to the north of ours. In 1933, my parents indirectly purchased about fifty acres from her. My parents did not wish to make the purchase directly because they felt Mrs. Lawless would charge the Lesser Lodge a higher price than she would a casual purchaser, so my Uncle Ben bought the land and transferred ownership to the hotel. That land had some of the best blueberry bushes ever picked. The campers would collect enough blueberries for the baker to make sufficient pies for all the guests, staff, and campers.

Mrs. Lawless did washing and ironing. One morning when I was 10 years old, my Cousin Bernie Rader and I were going to her house to deliver clothing that required her services. On the way there, we were accosted by two large barking dogs. Ordinarily, I would have run away, but I was afraid for my cousin, who is a year and a half younger than I. I picked up a large branch on the ground and charged the dogs. I was very relieved that the dogs

ran away from me and that my pants did not require washing.

That same cousin was a prisoner of war during World War ll. On November 6, 2007, he was awarded the French Legion of Honor—the highest award given by France to a foreign soldier. I, on the other hand, received nothing for facing those two large barking dogs.

My cousin Bernie Rader in France (1944)

Bernie recently e-mailed me the following story:

"I remember when I was around seven years old, you and I went during the evening to get milk from a farm. We came back on Route 52, and cars with bright lights and cars with regular lights passed us. You told me the cars with bright lights were kidnappers and I'd have to stand still and stiff so they would think we were telephone poles."

Bernie never thanked me for saving him from the kidnappers.

Bernard's sister, Gloria Rader Katz, relates the following story:

"My mother used to take me to Mrs. Lawless to bring my father's shirts to be laundered. One day my mother and I picked up five laundered shirts, and Mrs. Lawless said "That will be $2.50." My mother said, "Last week I brought you three shirts and you charged me 75 cents for all three. If anything, five shirts should be $1.25 or less." Mrs. Lawless said she charged more because she hated to do shirts."

MENDEL (1931)

My cousin Gloria Katz was also good enough to remind me of another individual we knew at that time—a man by the name of Mendel.

Mendel, who was black, performed at many of the hotels and rooming houses during the afternoon. He spoke and sang in fluent Yiddish. He always performed on the lawn and he did not have to ask for money. He was so good, the guests offered it!

Mendel entertained at the hotel for seven or eight years until 1938; then he disappeared. He was well versed in Hebrew. I think he may have been an African Jew, but I never thought to ask.

Perhaps he returned to Africa. Or perhaps he moved to Israel when Israel invited all the black Jews to become citizens. Sadly, I never knew.

CHRISTMAS (1931)

During the Depression, for the whole month of December, the main topic of conversation among all my classmates was Christmas. The kids spoke about the gifts they expected to receive and to which relative's

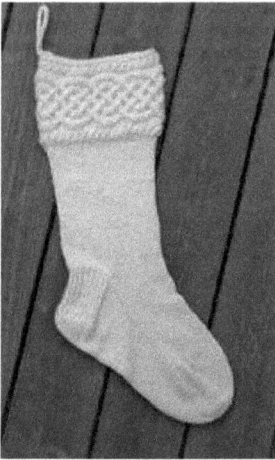

home they were going to go to celebrate Christmas Day. They discussed Santa Claus. Their mood was festive. On Christmas Eve, I was so imbued with the Christmas spirit, I hung my stockings on my room's front door in anticipation of Santa Claus. The following morning the stockings were just as empty as when I hung them. Apparently even Santa Claus was adversely affected by the Depression.

CASINO (1933)

In 1933, the Lesser Lodge had a "casino" built. In the Catskills, a casino is a place with a band and dance floor for dancing, a stage for entertainment, and a bar to quench guests' thirst and hunger. Sometimes gambling games were played.

The Lesser Lodge casino was erected on the side of a small hill. In order to make the floor level, the foundation and consequently the floor in the front of the casino were about nine feet higher than the floor in the back, which was about three feet below ground level.

Never reluctant to build rooms, my mother had four rooms built under the casino. Those rooms were used to house handymen and dishwashers and as storage facilities for the concessionaire. A fence was erected to protect the privacy of the four rooms under the casino.

A staircase built in front of the casino led to a landing that had one room on each side. Beyond the landing were the bar and a large dance floor. Beyond the dance floor was the stage with a small room on either side.

In order to build the bar, my brother-in-law, Herbert Auerbach, and I went to New Jersey to purchase glass bricks—the type which are seen today in many business establishments. A mason built a curved section made of the glass bricks. Then a carpenter followed the curve of the glass and constructed a wooden top. It made for a beautiful bar. Even a teetotaler would be proud to get drunk sitting in front of such a magnificent bar. The glass bricks we brought back then cost 35 cents each. Today such glass bricks cost between $7 and $10 each.

Herbert and Marilyn Lesser Auerbach with PFC Alvin Lesser

Max Rubinfeld, one of Lesser Lodge's athletic directors, and I shared a room to the left of the stage. Our room's window faced the main house. Max was a quarterback and a star player for Erasmus Hall High School. He was offered scholarships to many colleges. Instead, he went into the gasoline business and went on to become a millionaire.

As I mentioned, our room was below ground level and anyone could look into our room. Max was very handsome and a lot of women would stand looking through the window and talking to us. One day we decided to play a practical joke on them. While the women were looking and talking, we stood up, stark naked. We figured the women would start screaming and run away. Were we surprised! All they did was peer closer.

CASINO AND CONCESSION (1933)

One afternoon while I was walking from the pool to the casino with two young married women, we saw a body lying on the ground. Closer inspection revealed that it was a handsome red-headed handyman who lived under the casino. He was dead drunk. He was not clothed and his extremely well-endowed genitals were exposed. One of the women said to the other, "I'm going to have my husband dye his hair red and drink a lot more." She was kidding ... I think.

My uncle, Willy Margolies, was the hotel's first concessionaire around 1931. Because there was no casino as yet, his concession was built in a converted outhouse. The outhouse had been thoroughly cleaned and moved and filled and covered over. Whenever anyone would ask Willy, "How's business?" he'd say "It stinks."

After the casino was built, my Uncle Ben was the concessionaire and he had a crap table made from a converted pool table. Uncle Ben used to throw the dice and anybody who threw a higher number than he did would win an amount equal to the sum he had wagered. Everyone else would lose, including anyone who threw the same number as my uncle. To put this in gamblers' vernacular, the house had a 15-percent edge. I thought the people who played the game were nutty.

One season we had a guest who had a tattoo on his arm. Each night, in the casino, he would have a double shot of liquor, take a lit cigarette, and try to burn off the tattoo. The scar from the burned area looked worse than his tattoo.

THE CASINO BAND (1933)

After the building of the casino in 1933, the hotel started hiring bands for the summer. The band, generally made up of three or four musicians, played for the guests wishing to dance and for the enjoyment of the other guests. Before the show started, it was my job to line up the wooden folding chairs in rows facing the stage and then to remove them after the show. This became easier for me after the carpenters attached four chairs together using small strips of wood.

When we were young, I loved to dance with my sister Marilyn. She was a great dancer and could do the Lindy Hop as well as the best of them. But even then she would quickly get out of breath, I'm sure it was due to her smoking.

BAND AUDITIONS (1933)

Before each season, my parents would insist my brother and I go to audition the bands available to work at the hotel. Figuring out which band was best was difficult because my brother and I are both tone deaf. We would make feeble attempts to ask other listeners about the various bands' abilities. But in the end, we'd recommend to our parents the band which appeared to have the best personality.

When I was about 10 years old, my mother insisted I take saxophone lessons. I took lessons for three years for $2.00 a lesson. After three years, I had a terrific vibrato but I couldn't play two notes by ear. It was a waste of my parents' valuable money and my none-too-valuable time.

This was not the worst pain my mother inflicted on me. Two years earlier, my mother had sent me to the Brooklyn Museum to become a ballet dancer. I was eight then, and I was fat. When I ballet danced, even the teacher could not keep from giggling.

For its last ten years, the Lesser Lodge hired an excellent four-piece band under the direction of Leon Seaver.[19] They were able to accompany the singing entertainers without any problem and were more than capable of playing good dance music.

During the early years, once during each season, all the bands, including the Lesser Lodge band, played in the casino of a different hotel. The bands placed advertisements on telephone poles heralding this great extravaganza. The social directors, singers, and the rest of the entertainers accompanied their bands. At the end of the performance, the guests would be asked to financially reward the band and entertainers. The average salary of a band member was $12 a week. By doing this, the entertainment staff was able to earn a little extra money.

CASINO SOCIAL DIRECTORS (1933)

In the early years, social directors and singers were hired by the hotels to provide entertainment to the guests. They would be part of the staff and would live and eat at the hotel.

The social directors were the ones who planned the shows. They would tell the singers when they were to perform. If the social director was experienced, he would have material—skits, monologues, and games— to provide entertainment for several weeks. They would tell humorous stories and had to be able to sing.

At times, Lesser Lodge's social director would call on my brother-in-law, Herb Auerbach, to sing. Herb had a good voice and the guests, too, often asked him to sing. "Where or When" was their favorite.

It was one of the jobs of the social director to arrange horse races for the guests' entertainment. The guests would bet which horse would win the race. There would be facsimiles of six horses. The speed of each horse was determined by the roll of the dice.

Masquerade Night was a big hit with the guests. The guests came in all types of costumes—some good, some bad. The winners would receive a bottle of champagne as a prize.

At times, the social director would have an intermission to enable the guests to play musical chairs. The band would play and the people walked around the chairs. As the guests walked, one of the chairs would be taken away. The band would suddenly stop playing before the end of the song, and one of the walkers would be left without a chair and therefore he would be out. This would continue until there would be only one person able to sit. The one left sitting was awarded a prize.

Sometimes, as a joke, the social director announced the prize for winning would be a week's free board. When the contest was over, the director would present to the winner a weak board made from wood.

One season, a handsome fellow and his dog came to the hotel. He was driving a fine-looking convertible. He told my mother he was a social director and a magnificent singer. He complained he had a cold. For two days, he sang the scale beautifully but was unable to sing a song. My mother fired him. She also fired the dog.

Hispanic, black, and gentile singers performed at the hotel. Each and every one of them sang Mon Yiddisher Mama (my Jewish mother).

With the passage of time, the type of entertainment hotels like Lesser Lodge provided changed completely.

Two agencies, one owned by Jack Segal and the other by Charlie Rapp, began providing the entertainment. They hired comedians, singers, and dancers and furnished them with room and board. Most of the hotels and rooming houses started utilizing their services. Each night, these agencies arranged for their entertainers to go to two or more hotels to perform.

It was beneficial to the hotels because they were not required to house the entertainers nor did they have to be worried about the quality of the shows. The shows provided by either entertainment agency were almost invariably good. It was beneficial to the performers because they worked a double or triple shift and made more money. The Lesser Lodge retained the services of Jack Segal. When I was married, June 8, 1947, Jack provided entertainment as a gift.

In addition, the Stanley Wolf Players, a theatrical group made up of aspiring actors, presented a dramatic performance at the hotel once a week. These performances were always enjoyed by the guests.

In one of the Stanley Wolf shows, one of the actors was supposed to be taken off stage and shot. The sound of the shot was supposed to reverberate throughout the casino. Unfortunately, the off-stage gun did not fire. The actor who was supposed to do the shooting decided he had to ad lib. He screamed "I stabbed him to death." With that, came the resounding sound of a shot and boy did it reverberate.

The guests who came to the hotel were primarily married couples with their children. Economic times were not good and only infrequently would the husband stay all week, often leaving behind his wife and children to enjoy the relative coolness and the activities.

On Friday nights, the husbands returned to the hotel to spend the weekend. There were private parties and the casino was crowded. There were also many other joyous activities.

Casino, Labor Day Smorgasbord. Joseph Lesser is to the left of the cook, Evelyn Lesser, Marilyn Lesser Auerbach, and I are to the right of the cook. Guests sit at the bar in the background.

Each Labor Day after the show and dancing, the dining room staff would bring to the casino a great deal of food prepared by the cooks. Five or more tables, covered with special tablecloths and bedecked with ferns, would be used to hold the food. The affair was semi-formal and was greatly enjoyed by the guests.

CASINO NEW STAGE (1936)

The Lesser Lodge hired a stage builder in 1936. He changed the stage completely. He put new lights, both at the top and the bottom of the stage, plus a bank of colored lights on the ceiling in front of the stage that shined on the actors. In order to regulate the curtains and lights, there were 16 switches.

Runners and heavy front curtains were made. Around the rear and sides of the stage, thin black curtains were installed so that a person could walk or stand behind them and not be visible to the audience.

However, installing all this advanced staging equipment created a problem. The old-style cartridge fuses were in the cellar of the main house and they frequently blew, causing the casino to be left in semi-darkness. When that occurred, I was forced to run to the main house, pull out the dead fuse, and insert a new one. This took about 10 minutes. Later in the season, we had the electrician install a system that doubled the amperage, thus ending the unintended blackouts.

CASINO COMEDIANS

Many of the comedians who performed in the Catskills went on to become famous. Jerry Lewis[20], for example, performed numerous times. He was at that time employed by one of the hotels in the Catskills as an entertainer. There was a guest, Joe Kessler, who, together with his family, came to the Lesser Lodge for years. Joe made arrangements for Jerry to entertain at the Lesser Lodge.

Each time Jerry performed for the Lesser Lodge, he was paid $25. He would bring a record player, play the Jewish song "Romania," mime the words and dance around madly. Jackie Mason,[21] Alan King, Danny Kaye[22] and other popular entertainers also performed at the Lesser Lodge.

Buddy Hackett[23] performed at Lesser Lodge numerous times. Whenever he came, he would go to the casino and play the pinball machine for hours. Buddy had numerous routines and they were all great. He never used a dirty word at any of his performances at the Lesser Lodge. The dirtiest Buddy got was when he said "Use Preparation H and kiss your hemorrhoids goodbye," or "Do infants have more fun in infancy than adults have in adultery?" Later on in his career, for some reason, he started using filthy language. Buddy Hackett was so good at what he did; I never saw the necessity for profanity.

Buddy used to tell the story about the Catskill limousine driver who had made arrangements to pick up Mr. Sol Schwartz who had an 8:00 appointment. He then went to Brooklyn to pick up two more passengers going to the Catskills. The hackie then went to Mr. Sol Schwartz's house again to pick up Sol's sister, who had a 10:30 appointment. Buddy also gave a long monologue about Abraham Lincoln and "Useless" S. Grant. It was humorous and civil.

Alan King, another popular entertainer, told a story about the time he spent in Europe and how he'd gone to the ballet and watched the ballerinas dancing on their toes. He remarked, "I don't understand why they don't build the stage two inches higher." On another occasion, while giving a short summary of every Jewish holiday, King said, "They tried to kill us. We won. Let's eat."

BRONX AND BROOKLYN (1932)

After 1932, our family started living during the off-season in the Bronx and Brooklyn. We lived in the Bronx at 1205 Simpson Street, then in Brooklyn, at 621 Lefferts Avenue, 1010 President Street, and ultimately at 436 Eastern Parkway.

LAKE (1932)

When acquired, the Lesser Lodge had a brook flowing from one end of the property to the other. The brook continued under a bridge on Route 52. During the very early years, a makeshift dam was made on the other side of the bridge. This was on property owned by a Mr. Tremper. Mr. Tremper didn't mind us using his property.

The Gang and me at the new dam
First row: Claire Blatt, Marilyn Lesser
Second row: Me, Bernard Rader, Harvey Blatt
Rear: Unknown, Ann Stern

The lake created by the dam was about 20 feet by 30 feet, very small. But it served its purpose. The small number of guests the hotel then accommodated could go swimming and sit and talk on its banks. I learned how to swim in this little lake. Years later, when I attended Boys High School, I was on the swimming team.

I have always felt stupid when I tell people I attended Boys High School in Brooklyn. After all, I could have gone to Erasmus Hall High School, which was attended by girls as well as boys. To a degree, I atoned for my mistake by attending most of the dances at Erasmus Hall. I swam for Boys High and danced for Erasmus Hall.

In 1932, a large lake was built on Lesser Lodge property. We were fortunate enough to have a large mass of flat land through which a brook flowed. On either side of the brook the slope was steep, thereby enabling the building of a narrow, but quite tall dam. To strengthen it, truckload after truckload of dirt was placed in front of the dam until it was capable of holding back a huge amount of water. The dam had a screw wheel on top that was used to let the water out of the lake during the winter.

The new lake was large and could easily accommodate twenty rowboats, eleven more than we had purchased. It covered over twenty acres and took about eleven days to fill to overflowing. The dam's overflow ran south under a bridge on Route 52. It then flowed west and then northward into what was called "Kramer's Lake."

Lesser Lodge's new lake had a large beach area that was large enough to accommodate many guests. Beach chairs, tables, and umbrellas were placed in appropriate places. The day campers swam in an area on the opposite side of the lake.

Beach area shown in background. Campers swimming in foreground.

We all thought that in such a large lake, a float would be desirable, but no one knew how to build a float. So we improvised.

We first joined several boards together to create a six-foot by six-foot slab. Then on the four sides of the slab, we attached a six-inch piece of wood, even with the top of the slab but running down toward the water—this to keep four fifty-gallon air-filled drums in place under the slab. Lo and behold, we had a workable float!

Float and dock area

One day when I was driving over the George Washington Bridge—named in honor of his false teeth—I saw a rowboat lying on the side of the road. Where, I wondered, had it come from? Very few people row on a bridge.

It turned out that my brother Seymour had purchased nine rowboats and had rented a small truck to take them up to the hotel's lake. While on route, the rope holding the boats had loosened and one of the boats had slipped off the truck. When Seymour arrived at the lake, he had eight boats and an extra set of oars.

Seymour Lesser and wife Claire

My wife and I named our son Gary. Seymour and Claire named their daughter Jill. My sister Marilyn and her husband Herbert Auerbach named their sons Paul and David. They all went on to be great if somewhat mischievous friends. Gary and Paul were born four days apart in 1948. Stories about them abound.

For example, on one occasion, just two days before the Fourth of July 1958, when the hotel expected to have a full house, Gary and Paul, having nothing to do, decided it would be fun to let the water out of the lake so they could "shoot the rapids." They took one of the hotel's rowboats, placed it in the stream below the dam, and then turned the wheel on top of the dam, letting the water explode out of a 24-inch wide pipe that ran under the dam. The outflow of water was massive. Gary and Paul "rode the rapids" for a mile, ending up in Kramer's Lake.

The new dam on Lesser Lake shown in front of the boat docking platform. The handball courts and day camp are shown in the rear.

Apparently (we later learned), they had done this quite often. But this time they forgot to close the screw wheel. In about five hours, the entire lake had drained away.

The next morning Gary and Paul found themselves not only enrolled in, but moved to, Camp Chic-A-Lac located just a few miles away in Youngsville.²⁴ My father was in such a mood, he would prefer not to have waited until morning; he would have sent them in the dead of night. And this would have been easy as "Uncle Carl" Meltzer (as he was called) was the director of Camp Chic-A-Lac and a friend of my parents.

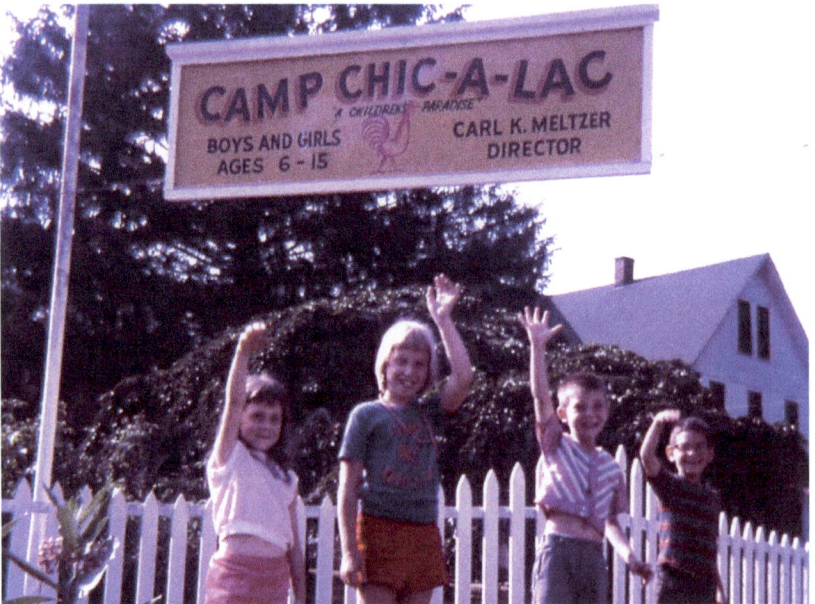

Camp Chic-A-Lac

My wife and I packed Gary a suitcase with several changes of clothing. At the end of the summer, Gary returned to us with the clothes he was wearing and only one sock.

Camp Chic-A-Lac insisted that their campers write to their family once a week. Perhaps fearing his parents wouldn't know from whom the letters came, he invariably signed his letters to us "Your Son, Gary Lesser." We would never have guessed he was our son unless he wrote "Lesser."

George Sewitt, the son of season regulars Irving and Jeannette Sewitt, was also a mischief maker. The three of them, Gary, Paul and George were inseparable friends like the Three Musketeers, all for one, one for all.

Irving, Jeannette, George and "Tippy" Sewitt

Kramer Lake was owned by a hotel west of the Lesser Lodge called Kramer's Hotel. The name was changed from Kramer's Hotel to the Union House to commemorate the unions that were being rapidly formed during this period and to lure union member guests. It later became Hotel Charles.

The Lesser Lodge was located between Midway Road and Lesser Lake (shown to the right). The stream connecting the Lesser Lake and Kramer Lake is shown.

THE BERGMANS (1935)

If there was construction planned, we would stay at the hotel during the winter. At times, during the winter, my parents visited Morris and Molly Bergman.[25] They had a home on Midway Road about three quarters of a mile north of the Midway School. They were very pleasant people, serving coffee and cake, and treated me amiably. I enjoyed their company. My feelings of loneliness lessened in their company.

Molly and Morris Bergman at The Midway (circa 1936)

In 2011, eighty years after having last visited the Bergmans, I received a telephone call from a lady named Alexis Bergman. She had discovered, in a roundabout way, that I was writing a memoir about the Catskills and that I knew the Bergmans, who were her grandparents. She informed me she was attempting to discover more about her grandparents. We exchanged photographs.

Alexis told me the reason the Bergmans bought a home on Midway Road was because of its high altitude and its curative effect on people suffering from lung problems. Alex, their son, had tuberculosis, and sad to say, he died of the malady at an early age, before he had the opportunity to live in his parents' new home. They took in summer boarders in their house and in a building that they called the "bungalow." They called their resort "The Midway."

Alexis at The Midway

The Bergmans had another son named Nathaniel. Nat married a girl named Francis. Nat and Francis are the parents of Alexis Bergman-Snyder.

The Lesser Lodge purchased its general hardware items at Frankel Hardware store in Liberty. I was surprised to learn the Bergman's daughter, Ida, had married Sidney Frankel prior to the opening of the store. All the years I shopped at their store, I was unaware of their relationship with the Bergmans.

The Midway (circa 1938)

THE HAUNTED HOUSE (1933-1963)

About a mile north of Route 52 on top of a large hill was an old abandoned house which we used to call the "haunted house." So no one need be frightened, let me advise you, it wasn't really haunted. Behind the walls there were newspapers dated in the 1850s. Amongst other items, they contained stories about the Gold Rush, the Missouri Compromise, and slavery. We never took the articles from the haunted house because we wanted future visitors to enjoy them.

THE MARILYN HOUSE (1933)

The first addition erected at Lesser Lodge was a two-story building named the Marilyn House, in honor of my sister. My sister was six years old at the time and I was 11. My parents said the Marilyn House sounded better than the Alvin House. I have always detested the name Alvin and I always introduce myself as Al. The Al House would have had a nice ring to it.

The Marilyn House

The rooms in the Marylyn house had good beds and mattresses as compared to the beds in the rooms in the main building.

EXPANSION OF DINING ROOM & LOBBY (1934)

When the property was purchased in 1923, there was a porch in front of the main house. In 1927, a dining room and eight rooms on top of the dining room were added. At that time, the porch was extended so that it fronted the dining room as well as the lobby.

Main Building prior to expansion

In 1934, supports were placed on the ceilings of the dining room and lobby facing the porch. The walls were torn down, thereby joining the living room and the dining room to the porch. The new area was finished off so that it matched the dining room and lobby. In effect, the lobby was made considerably larger and six more tables could be placed in the dining room. In addition, a children's dining room was constructed which abutted the east side of the kitchen. The children's dining room was large enough to seat fifty children.

Main Dining Room

HECTOR (1934)

Mrs. Hector, a widow, owned an eight-room house on the south side of Route 52, one-half-mile from the Lesser Lodge. When the Lesser Lodge was filled to capacity, we would advise incoming guests they would have to take a temporary room off the grounds, for one or two nights, at Hector's. During this time, they could take their meals at the hotel and enjoy all the facilities of the Lesser Lodge. When other guests departed, the incoming guests left Hector's and moved to the hotel. Because these incomers paid the full weekly price, we paid Mrs. Hector for the rental of their rooms.

Mrs. Hector had one son about whom I know absolutely nothing except he rode a motorcycle. But I do know he was a master of balance. He rode his motorcycle past the hotel at a rapid speed, standing on his head, legs extended straight up, with only his hands grasping the handles. That was quite a feat.

IRVING COHEN (1935)

Irving Cohen worked for the Lesser Lodge as a children's waiter. Irving had his girlfriend visit him on frequent occasions. He also had other girls visit him. I was only 10 years old, but he gave me tips on how to make love to a woman. When I was 10, I didn't know "why" I would want to make love to a woman. It didn't take me long to find out.

The experience Irving had at our hotel certainly stood him in good stead. Irving went on to become the dining room manager (maître d') at the Concord Hotel, the largest hotel in the Catskill Mountains. Valuable experience pays great dividends. Had he not first worked at the Lesser Lodge, who knows what his destiny might have been?

CONCORD HOTEL (1936)

Mr. Arthur Winarick, who owned the company that made Jeris Hair Tonic, built the Concord Hotel at Kiamesha Lake. He must have been a plain, ordinary man. I recall my parents taking me to the Concord to see Mr. Winarick, for what reason I don't remember, and we spotted a workman digging in the ground. We asked the workman where we could find Mr. Winarick. The man stood up from his labors and said, "I'm Winarick."

The Concord had a golf course called "The Monster." To play The Monster, you needed a set of golf clubs and a canoe. Due to the length of the holes and the amount of water on the course, even the professionals refused to play tournaments there. The caddies couldn't put a canoe in the golf bag. But I always played it without any fear and I always broke ninety. As soon as I got to 89 I quit, sometimes on the 11th hole and sometimes on the 12th hole.

BROOKLYN AND THE BRONX (1933)

I was a student at the Midway School for four years, until 1932. From then on, we spent most of the winters in Brooklyn or the Bronx. It was the worst of times; the Depression continued unabated. Most winters were spent away from the hotel only interrupted when building or preparing for the upcoming season.

In 1933, while I was experimenting with gasoline at the hotel, I set my sister's leg on fire. My mother was passing by and, seeing what occurred, grabbed my sister and placed her in a carpet lying nearby, thereby smothering the fire and preventing more serious damage. As it was, the damage was serious enough. My sister spent months in the hospital. She bore the scars, although greatly diminished by the passage of time, for the rest of her life.

Because my sister was in a hospital in the Bronx, the family moved to 1205 Simpson Street. We were very poor. Any profit earned by the hotel was reinvested into the hotel. I remember my father dunking a roll in his coffee for dinner so the family could have better fare.

DUDWEILER

Starting in 1933, at the end of each season, our steady truck man, Mr. Dudweiler, would bring his truck to the hotel for the purpose of taking the hotel furniture and the family to New York. The truck would be loaded so that the back could hold couches upon which the family sat. Mr. Dudweiler came late in the afternoon so we could arrive at our destination when it was dark. I suppose my parents were ashamed of seeing the family driven by truck and then seeing us unload furniture and taking it to a rented apartment. I don't know why they would have been ashamed. In the "elite" neighborhoods in which we lived, we could have come with a horse-drawn caravan. But we kids did not mind; we did not understand, and besides we had plenty of food and were quite comfortable on the couches.

The apartments rented by my father generally cost $50 a month, and there was usually a concession of one or two months for which he didn't have to pay. Most winters, the family lived in Brooklyn. When the season ended and we returned to the city, my parents took whatever food was left over for us to eat during the winter. One year there were many pounds of liver left over and the family had a steady diet of liver. For the rest of her life, my sister wouldn't look at liver, much less, eat it.

For several winters, our family lived at 1010 President Street at the corner of Franklin Avenue. There were two advantages for me; both my public school (P.S. 241) and my uncle's delicatessen, Ben and Sol's,[26] were nearby.

My public school career started out badly through no fault of my own. I had learned when you rapidly moved your hand in the direction of a boy's genitals he would flinch. After learning such a wondrous thing, I had to try it out. In all innocence, I did this to Dorothy, the teacher's pet, and all hell broke loose. The teacher, Mrs. Halloway, snapped, "Lesser, how can you do such a terrible thing?" and gave me a lecture and a sizable demerit. The news traveled rapidly. Another teacher, Mrs. Jones, stood me in front of the room, and for at least 10 minutes delivered such an abusive diatribe that it stunned me. I didn't know what I had done. I didn't know what she was talking about. After that, I became a marked man. By the way, Dorothy did not flinch.

One of my friends was named Bertha Jackson, the only black student in the school. She was pretty and was very nice to me. In the unsigned voting for Prettiest Girl at the School, I voted for Bertha Jackson. My vote wasn't even signed and the teacher blurted out, "Lesser."

My mother had to come to the school so often, the casual observer would think she was a member of the faculty. The teachers must have wondered how such a wonderful woman could have such a terrible son.

Even six years later, when my sister Marilyn started to attend P.S. 241, my tarnished reputation remained. My sister complained, "Because of you the teachers watch me like hawks and I get lower marks than I deserve." But the teachers soon discovered she wasn't as mischievous as I, and eventually even began to like her.

My uncle, who was half owner of Ben and Sol's delicatessen on Franklin Avenue, gave me a job working Sundays. I worked from 12 to 9 and received $3 for the day. Today I earn twice as much and don't have to work as hard.

Many Ebbets Field baseball players utilized Franklin Avenue on their way to the Franklin Avenue terminal of the IRT (Inter-Borough Rapid Transit). While working at the delicatessen, I had the opportunity to meet many famous members of the Brooklyn Dodgers. For example, I met Carl Furillo, and the great shortstop "Pee Wee" Reese, when they stopped at Ben and Sol's for a frankfurter or a sandwich. I attended the first game played by Jackie Robinson, the first African-American permitted to play in the major leagues.

"Pee Wee" Reese   *Jackie Robinson*

DRIVING (1934)

During the years I was a child, we had many chauffeurs. Some would work for one season but most of them stayed on for two or more seasons. The first chauffeur I remember was Bob. When he had time, he would tell me stories about a boy with a magical chair who could go all over the world.

As I got older, I would beg the chauffeur to let me steer the car. By the time I was 13, I could steer and drive. Since that time I have never had an accident caused by my bad driving. But then again all accidents are caused by only one of the two drivers and if you asked anyone involved in an accident, almost 100 percent would say the accident was caused by the other driver.

MY BAR MITZVAH (1935)

I had my Bar Mitzvah in 1935. My father was well schooled in the Jewish religion. He had spent his youth in Krakow, Poland, studying the Talmud. He had a good voice and knew how to blow the Shofar.[27] He performed the ritual service (officiated) at all Jewish holidays as well as my Bar Mitzvah.

In preparation for my Bar Mitzvah, I received two nickels each day to take the trolley car to the Lower East side to learn my portion of the Haftorah.[28] It took over 45 minutes to get to the rabbi who was to teach me. Unfortunately, I was tone deaf and when I chanted, it sounded like chalk scratching on a blackboard— maybe not even that good. The Rabbi, in order not to inflict torture on both of us, spent a minimum amount of time on the Haftorah. He was a brilliant man. He taught me grammar, about the subjunctive, perfect, past perfect, etc. Had I stayed with him longer, he would have taught me where to put commas and semi-colons.

I was Bar Mitzvahed at the Lesser Lodge. It must not have been a grandiose affair as I remember nothing about it, except gallantly struggling through the chanting of my Haftorah. How God must have suffered. I have a picture of me in my tallis (prayer shawl) the day I became a man. I look heavy and not nearly as handsome and charming as I turned out to be. My only fault, which you cannot see in the picture, was excessive modesty.

My Bar Mitzvah (1935)

I received various gifts to commemorate my Bar Mitzvah, one of which was a wristwatch. My parents were not engaged in any construction at the time and we moved to the city at the end of the season.

One day a man accosted me and said, "Would you like to earn a fast two dollars?" Two dollars was a fortune. Remember, at that time, a two-glass malted was only 10 cents. After I replied "yes" he said "Take this package to 909 Franklin Avenue, and they will give you a receipt. Bring the receipt to me and I'll give you the two dollars." I rapidly agreed. He then said, "I can't be sure you won't keep its valuable contents. Leave me your watch as security." I gave him my watch.

Needless to say there was no 909 Franklin Avenue. I rushed back to the man to tell him there was no such address, blithely unaware of my idiocy. Of course, there was also no man. When I opened the package, it contained old newspapers.

It cost me my watch but I learned a valuable lesson that day that has stood me in good stead. After that I never trusted anybody until I was positive he could be trusted, and I never entered a business transaction until I investigated all the details.

By way of example, I recently received a telephone call giving me the name of a prestigious organization advising me they were holding in escrow $2,829.39 that belonged to me. He said that I must send them a $97 filing fee and the escrow money would be sent to me. I told them to take the $97 out of what was due me and to send me the difference. The caller mumbled a few words and hung up. In my day, I've had many opportunities to make an ass of myself, but I have never taken advantage of them. I am not mule-headed.

Brooklyn Jewish Center

During the winter, when my parents were not running the hotel, my deeply religious father asked me to attend Hebrew school at the Brooklyn Jewish Center. He did not exactly ask; he told me, he insisted, and he demanded. I explained to no avail that my friends were in the school yard playing football and basketball. At the school I learned practically nothing because I wasn't interested. I do remember the name of my teacher, Mrs. Serbin, whom I liked very much. I asked my parents to invite her to the hotel gratis, but she never came.

To add insult to injury, my dad forced me to go to the synagogue every Saturday. May God forgive me, I wasn't religious then and I'm even less religious now. As a matter of fact, I thank God I'm an atheist. I still remember my dad standing with his back facing the pulpit whenever he disagreed with what the rabbi was saying.

The Alsyn (1935)

The next building erected at the Lesser Lodge was called The Alsyn in honor of my brother Seymour and me. The 20 rooms in the two-storied building were of good size and each room had an adjoining bathroom. The beds and mattresses were of good quality. Class had arrived.

The Alsyn

THE KITCHEN (1937)

In 1937, the original kitchen was dismantled and rebuilt, and the dining room was extended so that it could hold eight more tables and 64 more people. The walls were painted and a clear veneer was applied. All the lighting fixtures were replaced.

New dishes were purchased. The meat side of the kitchen was furnished with dishes which were white in the middle and had a red two inch border. The white center contained a red circle which had inscribed in white script "The Lessers." Few of these dishes remain but we have one in our home.

The dairy half of the kitchen had plain white dishes so that they could be distinguished from the meat dishes. The dishes were washed in two adjoining areas. The dishwashers were not too particular in regard to the cleanliness of either set of dishes.

The dairy side had a separate stove and grill which was used for the preparation of breakfast. There was a separate area used for the preparation of salads. Part of the kitchen contained a baker's oven.

I was given the job of buying a freezer, a dishwashing machine, and silver utensils. I saw an advertisement telling where kitchen items were to be auctioned. I went to the auction and the first thing being auctioned was a dishwashing machine. I figured the machine was worth about $500.

I kept on bidding until I reached $500. Someone else bid $550 and I stopped bidding. The auctioneer then announced some mistake had been made and the dishwasher would have to be auctioned off again, I purchased the dishwasher for $350 at the second dishwasher auction.

I learned the auctioneering business quickly. There were shills in the crowd whose business was to bid up the price so the auctioneer could make more money.

The auctioneer realized I was on to him and probably signaled the shills to cease bidding. A new Sherlock Holmes was born.

DUTIES OF A HEADWAITER

In a relatively small hotel in the Catskills, there is no maître d'. His duties are assumed by a headwaiter. The headwaiter arranges for the seating of new guests in accordance with the description he receives from the front office, e.g., male, female, young, old, middle-aged, and so on. The headwaiter earns the bulk of his compensation by working as a waiter. He hires the waiters and busboys, assigns them tables, and oversees their work.

At the Lesser Lodge, the most important duty of the headwaiter was to make salads for the afternoon and evening meals. Making 250 salads is not an easy chore, and the headwaiter called on the dining room staff to assist him.

KITCHEN—JACK BURNS

The Lesser Lodge retained the services of Jack Burns as headwaiter. He worked for many seasons until the hotel's demise. He was a nice guy with a good sense of humor. At his request, every Friday I went to a place where there were beautiful ferns. Ferns grow larger and nicer looking when they grow near water. I selected the prettiest, which the waiters would place on the table as decorations.

One summer, early into the season, Jack developed a boil on his behind. As the boil got larger, it became more and more painful and to Jack it was torture. Finally the boil burst—talk about happiness!

At times, I was assigned the job of buying chickens. I would go to Liberty to the "shochet." According to the kosher doctrine,[29] the shochet was the only one who could terminate the life of a chicken so that it was kosher and could be eaten by religious Jews.[30] He would take the chicken, remove some feathers from the neck and slit the chicken's throat with a sharp knife. He then placed the chicken on the ground. They walked around as if they didn't have a care in the world. Then they plummeted to the ground. I couldn't understand why killing a chicken in this manner was more humane than wringing its neck. Nor did I understand why it would be more kosher than a chicken killed in another manner. Religion certainly has its peculiarities.

PASSOVER (1938)

After the hotel grew in size and could accommodate more guests, the Lesser Lodge stayed open for Passover. My father officiated during the Passover dinners and took charge of the Morning Prayer service. The Lesser Lodge was usually very crowded at Passover because the people who came did not want to be bothered with the changing of dishes and all the other rituals the celebration involved.[31]

My dad is shown standing. To the right of the candles are my niece Jill, my son Gary, and my nephew Paul.

BED LUGGING (1938)

Most new guests arrived on Friday. My sister would furnish me the requirements of each room where changes had to be made to serve the needs of the new arrivals. With the help of a handyman, I would lug the beds from the storage room to each room per the instructions received from my sister. The beds that were to be replaced would be taken to a different room or back to the storage room. On too many occasions, the guests assigned to a specific room requested a different room. The lifting and lugging started all over again.

The beds, at that time, consisted of a small footer and a larger header. Both the footer and the header had each been welded with a vertical slot into which two railings were inserted, thereby making a bed. A bedspring and a mattress would then be put on the bed. The bedspring and mattress were barely adequate but in the 20s and 30s nobody knew the difference.

OH WELL (1938)

One year, in the midst of the season, the well which provided the water that was pumped into the holding tank went dry. It was calamitous—the hotel had no water. We had to carry buckets of water to cook, to wash the dishes and pots, and to enable the toilets to be flushed.

After three days, the plumbers rigged up piping from the lake to the water tank and installed a pump. It was a terrible three days of suffering. Luckily, the lake had pure, clean water. And, happily, the guests understood. That was not always the case.

Being in the hotel business meant dealing with many problems. Some guests complained the meat was too well done; others complained it was too rare, or that the dining room was too warm or was too cold.

JUPITER AGENCY (1938)

An employment agency named Jupiter Agency furnished the hotel with waiters and busboys. The job seeker paid the employment agency fee. With each new season, however, many past employees contacted the Lesser Lodge directly and saved the fee.

WAITERS (1938)

I became a waiter in the dining room when I was about 16. I slept in the barn with the other busboys and waiters. They were young and mischievous and played tricks on one another. One of the busboys was a sound sleeper. We tied a piece of thread to his penis and the other end to his wrist. We then made a great deal of noise until, finally, he awoke. I will always remember the expression on his face when he moved his wrist.

Practically all of the busboys and waiters were college students trying to earn enough money to pay their tuition. They did well. The waiters earned an average of $1,000 and the busboys earned about $700 during the season. Most of these young men ultimately became doctors, lawyers, accountants, and businessmen.

In those days, it was the duty of the waiters to wash and dry the silverware, clean the water tumblers, and set the tables. The busboys cleared the dishes off the table and took the dirty dishes to the meat or dairy dishwashers. Later, when the dishwashing machine had been set up, the busboys cleaned the debris from the plates and then placed them into the washing machine. The dishwashing machine was not at all interested in whether it was washing meat or dairy dishes.

The dining room and staff would shout to one another "5 and 3." This was a hint to the guests that $5 was a good tip for the waiters and $3 was a good tip for the busboys for a week's work. This was equivalent to today's "high five."

During the early years, the waiters went to the kitchen and loaded the dishes of food on their trays. The waiters took their trays laden with food into the dining room. Then the dish of food was taken directly from the tray and served to the guest.

The type of service changed as the hotel became larger and was able to accommodate more guests. Serving from trays was no longer in vogue. The waiters now used servers. The tray of food was placed on a server. The waiter would take the plate from the tray which remained on the server and serve each guest individually.

The server contained drawers for the silverware. One drawer was for the meat silverware and one drawer was for the dairy silverware. And God (and my father!) forbid if the two were mixed.[32] The rest of the server was used to hold cups, saucers, and underliners. Underliners are used when serving soup and smaller dishes to avoid the possibility of the waiter's thumb mixing with the food. After all, the hotel was kosher, and if you mixed dairy soup with a meat thumb, it would be a violation.

While I was working as a waiter, a mischievous guest asked me to permit him to run a thin hollow rubber tube across the wooden table before I put on the tablecloth. The tube permitted the passage of air. On one end of the tube was a small rubber ball that could be squeezed and the air from the ball would be forced through the tube. On the other end of the tube was a flat rubber bladder. When the ball was squeezed it would cause the bladder to inflate and deflate.

He placed the flat rubber bladder beneath the dinner plate of a girl he was trying to date. During dinner every time he squeezed the hidden ball, the girl's plate would rise and fall. The girl, of course, noticed the tiny rise and fall of the plate, but apparently didn't wish to make a scene

He also placed a small double-sided suction cup between her cup and saucer so that when the cup was lifted the saucer would come right along with it. I poured the coffee and when she went to drink, the saucer followed right along with the cup. I could see her pinky work to separate the cup from the saucer. After a few attempts to separate the cup and saucer, she looked up and everyone who had been in on the joke was laughing. She immediately realized what was going on and began to laugh. She was a real good sport. Later, I saw them dancing in the casino.

GOLDSTEIN FARM

The Goldstein Farm abutted the eastern border of the Lesser Lodge property. When I was six or seven years old, Mr. Goldstein and I took walks and he always called me *Yashka Guvnik*. I liked the man very much but he never explained what Yashka Guvnik meant in our language. He passed away at a very early age and I sorely missed him.

He left a wife and two sons. When his sons were about 17 years old, I asked them if they would like to work as busboys. I told them that when they were experienced, they would be able to work as waiters. They eagerly seized on the opportunity and worked for us several seasons.

Many years later, I visited their farm. The two busboys were then in their early 70s. We greeted one another as if we were family. They both were married and had grown children. I reminded them of how their father and I used to walk together with him calling me *Yashka Guvnik*. Neither brother knew what it meant.

THE CASE OF THE MISSING PILLOWCASE

One season the hotel hired a waiter whose name was Al. The headwaiter nicknamed him "Aza." In Yiddish, Aza means "such a," as in *aza putz*. He didn't seem to mind. The best I can say about him is he was a magnificent dancer. He didn't do anything special but he was beautifully graceful.

One day he said he had received a phone call that morning and had to go home immediately. He said he would return the same evening. I asked the switchboard operator if Aza had received a phone call that morning. She answered in the negative.

I immediately got suspicious. I watched him as he was getting into his auto to leave. I demanded that he open his trunk. When he opened his truck, I saw it was half full with sheets and pillowcases. We didn't fire him because when he was in the casino he danced with the guests and, other than being a thief, he was a nice guy. But we watched him.

THE RANCH HOUSE (1939)

The next building constructed was a 14-room structure named the Ranch House. My parents had named the first two houses constructed, the Marilyn and the Alsyn, after their children. I suppose they decided it didn't pay to have another child just to name a building.

The Ranch house was the ultimate in luxury; the rooms were fairly large and each had a private bathroom. Truly luxury at its finest!

ARTY LANDSMAN (1939)

Throughout the years, the Lesser Lodge employed chauffeurs. The cars they drove were old Packards, LaSalles, and station wagons. One of the chauffeur's jobs was to go to the Liberty Railroad Station whenever a train from New York was to arrive. He would shout "Lesser Lodge" and bring back any guests going to the Lesser Lodge. In order to get to the Liberty Railroad Station when coming from New York City, people had to take the Weehawken Ferry and then the Erie-Lackawanna Railroad, which has been out of service since the decline of the borscht belt. When I was a young child, my father placed me in a car on the Erie-Lackawanna Railroad. I was told to be sure to get off at the Liberty Railroad Station. The train used coal for energy. By the time the train arrived in Liberty, I was covered with soot.

One of my friends, Arty Landsman, was hired as a chauffeur in 1946. One night my mother met him coming out of the room of one of the female guests at 2:00 in the morning. My mother patted him on the back and said "good boy." From that time forward, my mother, when she wanted Arty, would announce on the hotel's loudspeaker, "Arty the chauffeur wanted; come out from wherever you are."

Another of Arty's jobs was to take my father shopping for food. They used to shop at Sachs Brothers for produce and at Max Etess for kosher meat. Max and Arty got very friendly. One day Max gave Arty, free of charge, a very large and thick steak.

The cook grilled the steak for Arty to eat the same day. As Arty was eating his steak in the kitchen, my father, passing by, saw this huge steak and took the steak into the dining room. Speaking into the microphone, in the middle of the dining room, holding the steak high, my father announced, "Ladies and Gentlemen, I want you to look at how well the Lesser Lodge feeds its help."

Arty met his future wife, Rosalyn, at the Lesser Lodge. As of the time of this writing, 2012, Arty is 94 and still going strong. He tells me his body is still supple and no part of it gets stiff.

One day Arty was taking the luggage belonging to a new arrival from the trunk of the house car, when suddenly the car started rolling backward. Having tremendous presence of mind, Arty threw the guest's suitcase behind the tire of the car, thereby stopping its rolling. The guest did not give Arty a tip.

After Arty and Rosalyn were married, they came to the Lesser Lodge on a vacation. Arty, Rosalyn, my wife

Evelyn, and I decided we would play golf on the Sullivan County Golf Course in Liberty. This nine-hole course is very hilly and challenging. As we came to the 7th hole, three of us teed off and Rosalyn was the fourth. As Rosalyn was about to swing her driver, a twosome approached and sat quietly on a bench.

When Rosalyn teed off, we all heard a loud click; we shielded our eyes to better see the ball in flight. As we were gazing, we heard laughter from the twosome. Rosalyn had hit under and to the side of the ball. The wooden head of the club hit a stone, which had made the click, and there the ball stood, perfectly balanced on the tee. Of course we joined the twosome in laughter.

On one of the other holes of the same golf course, our group was ready to tee off. But walking slowly directly in front of us were two deer, who insolently gazed at us, as if knowing they were safe since it was not deer hunting season. Back then, deer were a common sight in the area.

MEETING EVELYN (1940)

One afternoon, when I was approaching 19 years of age, as I was setting my dining room tables for dinner, I saw a beautiful young lady, 15 years old, walking across the porch. She had come to Lesser Lodge with her parents Harold and Dorothy Caplan. As soon as I was able to get near her in person I said, "We have a date tonight." And so we did. Evelyn and I were married in 1947, after I returned from World War II. However, many events were to transpire before we married.

ATHLETIC DIRECTORS (1940)

Ruby Klein was the hotel's athletic director in 1940. He was a member of the family owning *S. Klein-On-The-Square Department Store* on Union Square in Manhattan. Ruby was a football player and used to run for miles on the hills surrounding the hotel when he wasn't on duty. He was a friend and was very well liked. I felt terrible when he was killed during the war.

Handball courts shown before construction of day camp and staff quarters

Joe (I forget his last name), was also an athletic director. Joe was the best single-wall handball player in the country. He and I used to go to other hotels and try to hustle. We didn't play for high stakes. It was mostly for enjoyment.

The hotel had another athletic director who taught us how to eat lobster. He, my wife, and I went to a lobster house in Liberty. He told us the tentacles must be cracked and all the juice must be sucked out before eating the lobster. We have been avid lobster eaters ever since.

SWAN LAKE (1940)

When there was a shortage of datable girls in my area, I would go looking for an attractive girl with whom I could dance, talk, and so on. Heading to Swan Lake, which is about six miles from the Lesser Lodge, I'd go to either the Swan Lake or Stevensville Lake Hotel in my quest.

Stevensville Lake Hotel, Swan Lake, NY.

Sometimes if I met a girl that I liked, I would take her to Belle Barth Bar and Grill. At that time, Belle Barth (Annabella Salzman) was a well-known entertainment personality. Belle could sing good songs and she could also sing dirty songs. In essence, she sang good and dirty. At other times, I took my date to Singer's Restaurant where I knew most of the entertainers who frequented the restaurant. Afterwards, when I was lucky, I took them to other places.

Me and my wheels

GROSSINGER'S HOTEL (1941)

Grossinger's Catskill Resort Hotel was the most famous hotel in the Borscht Belt of the Catskill Mountains. During its heyday, it averaged 2,800 guests per week, had 35 houses, and owned 1,200 acres of land. Grossinger's was the first entity in the world to use artificial snow for skiing. On its walls Grossinger's had autographed pictures of hundreds of luminaries who had been guests.

I worked as a dining room captain, under Abe Friedman, the dining room manager at Grossinger's, during the summer of 1942. In the winter I worked as a model for Pratt Institute. I needed to earn money to pay for my college education at New York University.

During the time I worked as a captain at Grossinger's, one of the waiters and I had a disagreement. He insisted we go down to the cellar and fight. In my youth, I had played handball for six to eight hours a day and, as a result, I was very strong. The fight was over in short order.

As a direct result of this fight, I received my first furlough from the army while stationed at Fort Bliss, Texas. The waiter had sued Grossinger's for physical damages, and the attorneys needed me as a witness. The waiter lost the case and received nothing. But I got to relax.

While working at Grossinger's, I met and spoke with Jennie Grossinger's mother. We all called her Mama, but her real name was Malke. Jennie and Harry Grossinger had two children, Paul and Elaine. I met Paul several times, but I never got to really know him. I did get to know Harry, Jennie's husband. I met him several times at the golf course club house. We spoke about the trials and tribulations of the hotel business. He struck me as being a very sad man.

Max Etess, the kosher butcher located in Liberty, had three children, Joseph, Sylvia, and David. Elaine Grossinger married David Etess. Evelyn and I were invited to the wedding, but not because I had been a dining room captain. The Lesser Lodge was kosher and therefore purchased its meat from Max Etess, and as a result Max Etess invited my parents, my wife, and me.

David Etess was a doctor and had a good sense of humor. One sweltering day in the middle of the summer, David came to the Grossinger's golf course, carrying a set of golf clubs and wearing a huge fur coat.

By the way, even though Grossinger's Hotel is no longer in business, its golf course is still active and is still considered one of the finest golf courses in the country.[33]

While working at Grossinger's, I saw a show featuring Eddie Cantor (shown above left) and his protégé Eddie Fisher (shown to the left). Eddie Fisher later married Debbie Reynolds. Then they divorced, and he married Elizabeth Taylor (shown above). Eddie Fisher's taste in women was impeccable. My wife gave me permission to have an affair with Elizabeth Taylor, but with no other woman. Sadly, Elizabeth Taylor never took advantage of this wonderful opportunity.

When traveling to and from the Catskill mountains, the most popular rest stops were the Orseck Boys Restaurant and the Red Apple Rest[34] on Route 17. My father saw Eddie Cantor having a bacon and tomato sandwich at one or the other of these rest stops. He was dismayed that a fine Jewish boy like Eddie Cantor would eat bacon. Such a thing!

SWIMMING POOL (1942)

In 1942, my parents decided to have a large swimming pool constructed at Lesser Lodge. A decision had to be made as to where to put the pool. My mother wanted to place it next to Route 52 near the lake. There was a 150 yard stretch of flat land which led to the day camp, the handball courts, and the volleyball courts. I argued that the pool should be put in this area because it was much closer to the guest quarters. In addition, I argued, a pool in this area could be used by the day camp members, and the volleyball and handball players. My arguments were so convincing that the pool was placed next to Route 52 near the lake.

Road to Camp Lesser Lodge.

The land was excavated and the pool was made of cement. The 10 feet bordering three sides of the pool and the 20 feet near the entranceway were also paved. The road leading to the day camp, as well as the swimming pool alongside Route 52, can be seen in the previous picture.

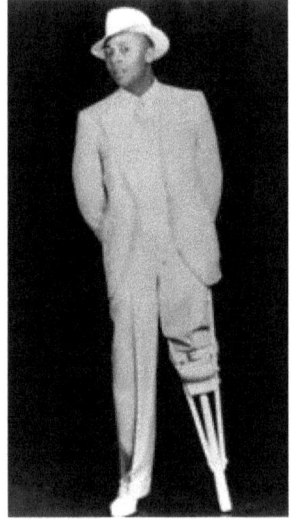

Peg-Leg Bates

At times the band played at the pool and the guests had the opportunity to dance in their bare feet. Other entertainers, such as Clayton "Peg Leg" Bates,[35] performed at the pool. Peg-Leg Bates had one wooden leg, but he sure could tap dance. He was a renowned entertainer in the Catskills.

Lesser Lodge advertisements set forth that the pool was "Olympic-sized." It wasn't. But it was a large pool—40 feet wide by 100 feet long. There was a one-meter diving board. The diving area was 10 feet deep. At the end of the season, the pool water was drained into the stream below the dam of the lake.

Wooden recliners were purchased for the guests to sit on and sunbathe, and umbrellas were supplied for shade. The entire pool area was surrounded with grass and was enclosed with a heavy wire fence.

On the side facing the dam, a large room made of cement was constructed. This room contained three huge tanks and all the equipment needed to chlorinate, purify, and circulate the water.

The Swimming Pool

Here's an interesting anecdote my sister Marilyn told me. They tried to keep Pop off the hotel's telephone reservation line because he had such a thick accent. But one day he answered the phone (it was before we built the pool). A lady asked "So, do you have a casino?" Pop said "Yes." She said, "So, do you have a day camp?" Pop said "Of course." She said "So, do you have a svimming pool?" Pop said "Vy, do you svim?"

MILLIE (1942)

During the season of 1942, I again worked as a waiter at the Lesser Lodge. I discovered I could earn more money at my parents' hotel. That was when I met Mildred "Millie" Katz. Millie was beautiful, full-figured, black-haired, and had skin as white as snow. She and her sister had rented a house in White Sulphur Springs, about a mile to the east of my parents' hotel.

Every day she walked from White Sulphur Springs to the hotel and helped me set my tables. Afterward we would dance in the casino and watch the show. Then I would either walk her to her home or I would take the house car and drive her home, albeit somewhat circuitously.

Once, in the late afternoon, I was walking Millie home and four fellows on the porch of the Leona Hotel in White Sulphur Springs started to badger us, making uncalled for remarks. I am sure they were jealous because this wonderful girl selected me instead of one of them. I suppose I should have invited them for a face-to-face meeting and administered a thorough thrashing. But, not having suicidal tendencies, I continued walking with Millie.

Millie lived in the Bronx and we met frequently in Manhattan. We got along extremely well until the night before I was inducted into the army. We then had a severe disagreement. I knew her address and I had given her my army address.

I loved Millie and I desperately hoped she would write to me but I was too stubborn to write to her. I have never seen her again. Many times I have thought about what could have been.

Sister[36] (1943)

By the time she was 16, my sister Marilyn was a competent business woman. She handled all the hotel's mail and spent hours on the phone speaking to potential guests. Many of them came to the hotel and my sister, in her inimitable manner, would convince them they had rediscovered Shangri La. She was superb at what she did. She also had a magnificent sense of humor.

After the demise of the Lesser Lodge, my sister worked for the Raleigh Hotel. She then received a better offer from Harriet Ehrlich, the owner of the Pines Hotel in South Fallsburg.[37] Marilyn worked for Harriet for years and they were great friends.

The Pines Hotel managed to stay in business until 1998, paid off all its creditors, and then closed its doors. In the 60s, my son Gary worked at the Pines Hotel (among others) for several years as a busboy and waiter. Like all good hotels in the Catskills, eating was the main activity. Harriet and Jerry Ehrlich now live in Naples, Florida.

My sister was a wonderful woman and I loved her dearly. She passed away in 1993. Had she not smoked, I feel she would be alive today. Marilyn passed away in my home, but to the bitter end she had to have "another drag" of her cigarette. I had her tombstone engraved "Mother, Grandmother, and Grand Person."

ARMY (1943-1945)

I served in the armed forces for three years, three months, and three days. I don't remember how many minutes. I started my army career at Fort Bliss (certainly misnamed) in an anti-aircraft battalion. I scored well on some tests and was transferred to the Army Student Training Program. I attended the University of Mississippi while I was in the ASTP. Later I became a navigator in the Air Corps. After the Battle of the Bulge I was transferred to the Cannon Company of the 71st infantry division. I then spent two years fighting through the hedge groves of France and mud in Germany. I received no medals, just a pension from the government for injuries I suffered.

THE DAY CAMP (1946)

The Lesser Lodge day camp was magnificent. It was built behind the handball courts some distance from the hotel so that the parents and their children didn't come into contact until the end of the day.

Evening Taps at the Day Camp

Joe Steinhart, a high-school principal, was in charge of running the day camp. He worked the camp for about 10 years. Joe was a very personable man; he often told interesting stories during campfire nights. The campers had their meals at the day camp. Breakfast was made at the day camp. Lunch and dinner were brought from the kitchen at the main house to the kitchen at the day camp.

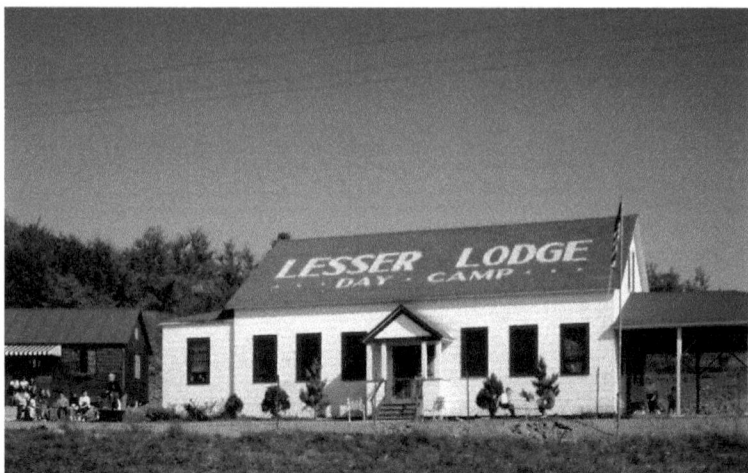

Lesser Lodge Day Camp. Arts & Craft Center on left

The camp had its own cook, "Mr. Allen," who reheated the food and prepared it for serving. It was the only name he ever had. He was very kind to my son Gary and to my nephew Paul.

Every morning at 8:00 a.m., all the campers would assemble outside of the main building and be led down a path to the camp, which was about 150 yards away. That's not entirely true—Gary and Paul were frequently late for camp; sometimes they never arrived. When Gary and Paul arrived at camp late, Mr. Allen always made them breakfast. He was very fond of the kids, and they were very fond of him. Mr. Allen was the only cook the camp ever had. He was a kind and gentle man. The campers would be returned to their parents at 5:00 p.m., generally at the swimming pool. Weather permitting, the campers were brought to the pool twice a day for a swim. At 6:30 p.m., the campers assembled again and were brought back to the camp for dinner and singing. In the evening, the campers gathered around the flagpole near the lake for "taps" and were then brought back to the hotel. As the guests were leaving the main dining room after dinner, their children would be in the lobby to greet them.

There was a separate house for arts and crafts. "Birdie," the arts and crafts teacher, lived in a partitioned room that was inside the cabin. Parents were charged for the materials used in the arts and crafts house. Campers made baskets and lanyards and worked in other media. There was a lot of entertainment provided for the children. Hayrides and horseback riding arrangements were made. Over time, more and more guests were coming to Lesser Lodge because of its day camp, which could care for close to 75 children.

When they tired of camp, Gary and Paul disappeared, usually with Gary's dog, Twig. They generally stayed well-hidden and away from the guests. There was a place in the back of the lake and beyond a beaver dam where Gary and Paul hung out, catching fish and salamanders and searching for that perfectly shaped flat rock for skimming on the lake. They called the area Ping-Pong Island.[38] When they weren't there, they were usually causing mischief somewhere else.

Gary and Paul played the pinball machine "Palisade's Park" a lot, as if it needed feeding. My mother was a constant source of nickels. The concession owner received a cut of the action from the pinball machine and jukebox. Gary and Paul placed "monkey dishes" under the front legs of the pinball machine, as if defying gravity. It slowed down the action and, as a result, they won many free games. Monkey dishes are dishes shaped like a soup bowl, but smaller.

Mattresses were sometimes stored in one of the four rooms beneath the casino; it was the perfect place for the boys to play "king of the mountain" after the concessionaire chased them out of the casino. At night they danced with the girls in the still of the night.

Gary and his dog Twig grew up together. Twig was very protective and didn't care much for mailmen and people in uniform. After Twig bit the mailman twice, the insurance company advised us they would cancel our household insurance if Twig was not removed from the premises. I begged my sister to take Twig. I told her our family would be heartbroken if Twig had to be put to sleep. My sister, Marilyn, lived in Liberty, six miles from the Lesser Lodge, and took the dog in.

The first night after giving Twig a new home, my sister called Evelyn, my wife. Marilyn told my wife that she was so frightened she was standing on the kitchen table with Twig below growling at her. My wife told Marilyn not to be silly; the dog was merely talking to her.

After that escapade, Marilyn loved Twig as much as we did. When the veterinarian told her he might have to remove the dog's testicles, my sister told him, "You remove the dog's testicles and I'll remove yours." That's love!

The hotel had a loudspeaker system for paging. When the dog heard its name over the loudspeaker, Twig, to the amazement of all the guests, would run to the front office. The dog is buried on the shores of Lesser Lake.

DAY CAMP HANDBALL COURTS AND HORSES (1946)

I was an avid handball player and loved the sport. I played four-walled handball at the Brooklyn Jewish Center and played with some of the best players in the United States. I played with Sid Luckman; he was one of the most famous Jewish quarterbacks in the National Football League. He said to me, "Why do you hit the ball so hard. It's better to play with your head." I told him "I can't get a handball glove on my head."

I convinced my parents that having handball courts at Lesser Lodge was an absolute necessity. They acquiesced and told me to find the proper person to build the courts.

Sid Luckman

I found the perfect person in Ferndale, close to Grossinger's Hotel. I don't recall what he charged, but he built four handball courts, complete with a macadam surface. Huge telephone poles were used to support the giant structure. The courts rivaled Fort Knox in strength, and they are still standing.

My parents utilized the strength of the handball courts by building rooms using the back of the courts as one side of the rooms. The rooms were sturdy and were used by the day camp personnel. Eventually, Gary and Paul had their own room at the camp.

Many of the children went on hayrides. The hotel hired a farmer to fill one of his large wagons with hay and come to the day camp. Twenty-five or more children went on a long hay ride. The day camp cook would furnish water, soda, and lunch.

Once a week, a young woman would bring five or six saddled horses to the day camp. The older children would be able to horseback ride a half hour for 50 cents.

I enjoyed displaying dominance over horses. One day as I was making a right-angled turn, the horse slipped and fell on its side. The horse did not land on my leg, but it could have. I remembered Benjamin Franklin's saying, "An ounce of prevention is worth a pound of cure," and decided to be less dominant with horses. I phoned the lady who brought the horses and asked her if the horse was okay. She told me he was "in stable condition."

TENNIS & VOLLEYBALL

The Lesser Lodge had a tennis court that had been built in 1928. It was made of red clay and had all the accoutrements.

Tennis court alongside Route 52 before construction of pool. Casino shown beyond parking lot.

In all the years of its existence, I never saw anyone playing on the court except for Mr. and Mrs. Steinhart and their son Casey. The tennis court was located just east of the Casino and next to the not-yet built swimming pool. When the swimming pool was put in, it was necessary to do away with the tennis court.

In front of the handball courts, which faced southeast, was a large area of flat land on which there was a volleyball court, an archery range, and shuffle board courts. The courts were used by both the adults and the children of the day camp.

The archery range

BASEBALL FIELD (1947)

The Lesser Lodge had a baseball field built in 1947. It was literally cut out from the side of a hill. The dirt bulldozed from the hill was moved to the lower part of the hill, in essence making a 50-yard flat surface. The charge for this service was $75 a day, and since it took about nine days, the total cost was $675. We then had our plumbers from Jeffersonville construct a fine backstop made of pipe and heavy wire.

A handyman attached four two-by-four pieces of wood together. After being attached, this formed a heavy block of wood that measured eight inches by eight inches by 15 feet. The block of wood was attached to a jeep. The handyman drove round and round the flat area and made it smooth. It turned out to be a good baseball field.

The hotel staff, the guests and I frequently played together. We often competed with other hotels on their baseball field, or would invite the baseball team of another hotel to play our team on our field. There was a strong competitive spirit and many people came to cheer on their hotel's team.

DISCHARGE

I was discharged from the army in March of 1946 and immediately joined the "20-20 club." The government gave me $20 a week for 20 weeks for surviving the war. This was an improvement. Before the war, I earned only $12.60 a week at Barth-Feinberg of New York City delivering musical instruments.

I didn't mind delivering piccolos and even saxophones. But one day they gave me a drum to deliver during rush hour and I had to take an I.R.T. subway train. As I was carrying the drum, I was struck by a mass of humanity. I could not move in any direction. "That did it!" I quit the next morning.

Being a veteran, I was entitled to certain benefits. One of the benefits permitted me to attend college at the government's expense. At that time, the cost was only $19 per credit hour.

During my second semester, I was stricken with jaundice. My doctor had me taken to the hospital where I remained for a month. Having nothing to do in the hospital but study, I learned more about my major, accounting, than I could have learned in years at college.

As a result of the studying I did in the hospital, my son Gary and I wrote a book titled, "Basic Accounting Simplified," when I was 89 years old.[39]

MARRIAGE

I had been going rather steady with a lovely girl named Shirley during the time I attended New York University. After being discharged from the hospital, having recovered from jaundice, I learned that my mother and my sister had been conspiring against that relationship. Not particularly caring for Shirley, they invited Evelyn—the girl I had been going with five years previously—to our home. As a result, Evelyn and I took up with one another again, started going steady, fell in love, and were married June 8, 1947 at the Commodore Hotel in Manhattan.

Evelyn and I visited Niagara Falls for three days during our honeymoon. We then went to the Green Mansions Hotel where we were to spend 11 additional days. Toward the end of our honeymoon, my mother phoned me and told me I was desperately needed at the hotel. I was never desperately needed by anybody in the past, so Evelyn and I cut two days off our honeymoon and went to my parents' hotel. I never did discover why I was desperately needed. Evelyn and I have been happily married for four years; four out of 62 isn't bad! Fifty years later we again went to Niagara Falls. Every 50 years, like clockwork, we go to Niagara Falls.

Evelyn has been with me through thick and thin. She stood by my side when I had jaundice, she was there when I had my hernia operation, she was there when I had a bout with depression, and stayed by my side when I had a minor stroke. Boy is she bad luck!

Kitchen and Dining Room Enlargement (1948)

In 1948, the hotel's old kitchen was dismantled. The ground beneath the kitchen was excavated to serve as a cellar and a foundation, and a much larger kitchen was built. The hotel being kosher, the kitchen was divided down the middle; one half was for meat and the other half was for dairy.

The dining room was extended again and permitted the hotel to install 10 more tables, which would hold an additional 80 people.

Like locusts descending and ravaging a field, flies regularly invaded the dining room. Screens on the windows were no barrier. The guests used to come and go. The flies only came. Every two or three days it was necessary to spray the dining room with Flit, a fly poison. Spraying was the only way to keep the number of flies under control. A few hundred strips of flypaper hung from the ceiling in the kitchen.

In 1952, a large Chrysler air-conditioning unit was installed in the dining room. It kept the dining room cooler but it really was inadequate. As soon as lunch was finished, my father would turn off the air conditioner because it cost too much to keep it running through the afternoon. And why make the dining room staff the least bit comfortable? In later years, air conditioning was vastly improved and window air conditioners were used to cool individual rooms. Finally, whole buildings were able to be cooled with central air conditioning.

BARN DEMOLISHED (1949)

In 1949, in order to have land on which to construct a new building, it was necessary to do away with the barn. All of the lumber used to build the barn was sold. The purchasers of the lumber did the dismantling, so it cost the Lesser Lodge nothing. The land was bulldozed, leveled, and on that land a bungalow was built. Later, the bungalow would be moved up the hill and a new building (to be called the Sheldon House) was constructed.

QUONSET HUTS (1949)

Prior to the dismantling of the barn my parents purchased Quonset huts to house the employees who were to be dislodged when the barn was dismantled. A Quonset hut is a metal building which looks like a can that has been cut in half.[40] It had room enough to comfortably place a double or two single beds.

One season the hotel hired a dance team. They were given a Quonset hut in which to sleep. The female member of the dance team complained they couldn't sleep in one Quonset hut because they weren't married. My mother said, "Don't give it another thought; I'll have it fixed by the time the show is over." Mom solved the problem by having a handyman hang a sheet down the middle of the hut. It should be noted the male member did not complain.

After my honeymoon, I resumed my duties at the hotel. Evelyn and I lived in one of the Quonset huts. I had a shower installed and it was quite comfortable.

One year we decided to have some relatives and friends over to celebrate Passover. For the occasion, we purchased lobster, shrimp, and other unapproved Passover goodies. As we were dining in this elegant manner, my father, who is very religious, walked in, surveyed the scene, and walked out. We were doomed and would never go to Heaven. But we had one hell of a good time.

NORMAN MARGOLIES (1950)

Norman Margolies, my cousin, was born with a great sense of humor. He spent many seasons at the

Lesser Lodge. Nothing ever interfered with his desire and capacity to do humorous things.

One morning at 2:00 a.m., Norman (shown in picture) turned on the hotel's loudspeaker and boldly announced "Ladies and gentlemen, breakfast is now being served in the main dining room. The waiters, the busboys, and the cooks are awaiting your arrival." By the time he finished his announcement, he had all the guests awakened wondering what was going on.

The next morning my father accosted him and said, "Are you out of your mind? There must be something terribly wrong with you. How can you wake everyone at 2:00 in the morning?" Norman apologized profusely. He kept on telling my father how sorry and embarrassed he was. He told my dad that it had been a terrible thing to do. He said "Uncle Joe, I did something stupid and I'm sorry."

The next morning at 2:00 a.m. Norman turned on the hotel's loudspeaker again and announced, "Ladies and gentlemen, yesterday morning I woke up everybody announcing breakfast; I am terribly sorry and I wish to take this opportunity to apologize to everyone I disturbed by my previous announcement."

Norman tells the story of the time he helped out the bellhop who worked in the children's dining room. The bellhop's job was to serve coffee, tea, and cookies to the guests after they left the casino and were preparing for bed. To impress the bellhop and educate him in the methods to be used in order to make money, Norman placed five singles in a cup. After they were finished rushing around and taking care of the many guests they had to serve, there were only two dollars in the cup.

My cousin Norman never got perturbed. The next night the bellhop served and Norman watched the cup. He said "The worst they could do now is to come out even."

Norman and Morty Seigleman, the athletic director, shared a small room to the right of the stage in the casino. One night Morty heard noise coming from the front of the casino. He took his bow and arrows, which he used to entertain the guests, and started shooting arrows to the front of the casino, which was about 50 feet away. Norman said, "Morty, are you crazy, you'll kill someone." Morty answered, "No one, but no one, comes into my room without knocking." Morty's room was about 1/50th the size of the casino.

DRIVEWAY (1950)

The old driveway started at Route 52 and proceeded straight up the hill to a parking area next to the office. The parking area was not large enough, and it was ugly.

To replace the parking area, a cinder block free-form was built by the masons and finished off so that it could hold water. It had two levels and falls. The water from the lower level would be pumped to flow over the falls onto the upper level and then flow to the lower level and into a pool filled with goldfish. The cycle was constantly repeated. Large lights were installed and the overall effect was beautiful to behold. The water at the bottom of the pool did not freeze during the winter and the fish were able to be recycled each year.

At the same time the modernizations of the lobby, card room, and dining room were being done, a new macadam driveway was built. The new driveway was semi-circular in shape. It started at Route 52 and proceeded in a circular manner to the front door of the hotel and then connected again to Route 52. Under the new arrangement, when a guest arrived, his luggage was removed by the bellhop, who would then drive the car to the parking field.

The parking field was located in front of the Quonset huts and could easily accommodate 150 cars. The west end of the parking field connected to Midway Road not too far from the bottom of the big hill. The area had already been leveled when the Quonset huts had been purchased and set in position. Since the ground was very hard and pebbled, there was no need for macadam to be laid.

This arrangement was very convenient for the guests because they did not have to walk as far to get to their vehicles.

FIGHT (1950)

One day my sister came and told me that a stranger on horseback was trampling our new macadam driveway. I rushed out to the horseback rider and excitedly told him to get off the driveway and never come back. He refused. I pulled him off the horse and we began fighting, rolling down the hill, across Route 52, until we were stopped by a barbed wire fence. I tried to pull the barbed wire across his face, but before I could do so, we were pulled apart by saner heads. He never came back.

THE BEAUTIFUL MILES (1953)

The family of Jack and Jean "Gina" Miles called themselves the hotel's "token gentiles." Jack was very Irish and Gina (shown to the left) was very Italian. Jack (shown on next page) owned a General Tire dealership in Freeport, New York.

Gina was a guest of the Lesser Lodge for over nine seasons and often brought their children, Helen Ann, Christine, and Jackie. All of them loved the hotel and the other guests couldn't help but love them. Gina and her children attended Gary's Bar Mitzvah.

The amazing part is the physical appearance of the Miles family. Gina and her daughters are beautiful; I mean drop-dead Hollywood beautiful and the men are handsome. Even Gina's grandchildren are beauties. I know because we have been very good friends for 60 years.

One Saturday my father was conducting Saturday morning Jewish services at the hotel. There were only nine men and by Jewish law 10 men are required for a minion. My father spotted Jack, Gina's husband, and not knowing he was a gentile, asked him to be the 10th. Jack didn't know what was going on and agreed. He wore a tallis and did what everyone else was doing. Despite this, Jack remained Irish.

Gina had a very pleasant singing voice. She was once asked to go on stage and sing to the audience in the casino. She said she was too timid to sing on the stage but she would sing behind the stage curtain. In the evening, the band started to play the song she was supposed to sing. When it was time for her to sing, she stood petrified and was unable to make a sound, much less sing a song.

Gina tells the story of when she was first married. Jack had opened a $500 checking account for her and given her a checkbook bearing her name. Gina was thrilled and bought a piano and other equally important necessities. Later, Jack informed her she had written a check and it had "bounced." Gina said, "How could that be, I still have blank checks I haven't used yet."

I recently received the following note from Christina ("Chrissy"), Gina's daughter:

Summers Spent at Lesser Lodge

Hi, my name is Christina Lucia Miles Reichenbaum and I would like to share with you some of my fondest childhood recollections that took place at the Lesser Lodge from 1956 to 1960.

I can never forget the smell of fresh baked rolls that permeated the crisp morning air as we would descend a winding road and many steps into the dining room!

Mr. Allen, the camp cook, was so full of life, always a big smile, and oh, was his corn soup delicious!

I remember Pop Lesser making his Friday night announcements over the loud speaker in his thick accent "The time to light candles is now."

I remember frozen Milky Ways that I would snatch up at the canteen when my mom was buying beer for her hair treatment.

There were a lot of good-looking people at Lesser Lodge. The ladies dressed to the nines in the "ensemble" of the day. Beehive hairdo's and lots of hairspray.

The shows that we put together, "Oklahoma," "South Pacific," "Damn Yankees," "Cinderella," were just a few that stand out as nothing short of spectacular, with everyone participating in some way.

All the children went to day camp while our Mom, single during the week (Dad came for the weekend), lounged at the pool and flirted with all the gorgeous young waiters. I remember the tree house on the mountaintop behind the day camp and the nearby blueberry fields. We would pretend Peter Pan lived in the tree house there and we got lost for hours.

I loved rowing on the beautiful lake and chasing frogs.

The relationships that we had with the Lesser and Auerbach families, which have endured for decades, were made closer because of the many summers that we spent together at Lesser Lodge!

Attending Gary's and Paul's Bar Mitzvah at Lesser Lodge, an unforgettable extravaganza!

Those times will always be very special to me and I will always cherish the innocence of it all! It was all good clean fun and spending time with good friends and creating lasting memories.

Thanks for the memories,

Christina Lucia

Christina Lucia Miles Reichenbaum

In one of my phone conversations with Chrissy, she reminded me of something that occurred during 1967. Our neighborhood, where Gina, Chrissy, John Paul ("Little Jackie"), and Helen Ann also lived, had been plagued by a Peeping Tom, no doubt because of the beauty of Chrissy and her older sister Helen Ann. She said, "Uncle Al, you and your sense of humor. My sister and I have been laughing through the years over your solution to the Peeping Tom problem. You said we should stand naked in front of the bedroom window and you would stand outside the window, hidden from view, and apprehend the Peeping Tom when he approached and call the police."

Jackie Miles

Another incident with the Peeping Tom occurred during one of my sister Marilyn's visits to our home in Wantagh. I was toweling myself dry when my sister screamed, "Someone is looking through the bottom of the curtains in my bedroom!" Wearing just a towel, I immediately rushed through the front door and began chasing the man, leaping over bushes and hedges like Superman. In mid-flight I thought to myself, "am I crazy? The police will lock me up for indecent exposure!" I did not catch the man but I made a valiant effort. The Peeping Tom was eventually caught by the police.

Helen Ann Miles

June Rader

TELEPHONE CALL (1954)

June Rader spent an entire summer at the Lesser Lodge in 1954. Her husband Bernard Rader came up weekends. June sent me an e-mail describing an incident. Here is what June wrote:

Labor Day came and there was going to be a big party and a midnight supper at the Lesser Lodge and I did not have anything appropriate to wear. My mother-in-law, Eva Rader, and I went to Liberty and brought back some black velvet material. She made me a black strapless dress that would be appropriate for the Labor Day affair and for any wedding.

However, I didn't have dressy shoes to go with such a fine dress. At that time, it was very expensive to make a long distance phone call. I called my husband's number, person-to-person, and asked to speak to Mr. Hy Blacksuede. Bernie got the message and the next weekend he brought up my dressy high-heeled black suede shoes. I never forgot how we laughed about that.

THE FINAL RENOVATIONS (1956)

After the construction of the Sheldon House, it was decided to beautify the important rooms, and an architect named Mr. Kagan was brought in to make the alterations. His changes included:

The Lobby. The architect threw out almost the entire contents of the lobby. The floor was carpeted; the ceiling was done over—painted and trawled—which looked lovely. A free-form brick enclosure was made. It housed flowers and contained a fountain that continuously changed the color of the squirting water. Large new glass windows were ordered and installed complete with curtains. New furniture was acquired and the entire front façade of the office was covered with white brick slabs. Swinging doors were made for the new driveway being installed. For the safety of the guests, asbestos was sprayed on the ceilings.

The Card Room. Because the day camp fed the children, the children's dining room was no longer needed and was converted into a card room. The ceiling was painted black, white lights were affixed to the ceiling, the walls were painted white, and the floor was covered with diamond-shaped black and white tiles. Club, diamond, heart, and spade shapes were made of plywood and painted red or black and affixed to the walls. The table tops were all white, and surrounding the tables were black leather chairs.

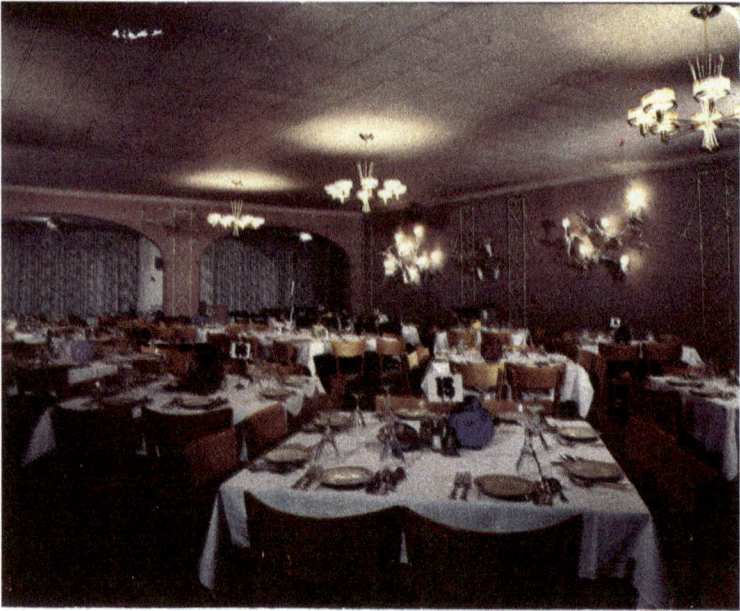

Dining Room. The walls were scraped and varnished. New lights were installed and new comfortable chairs were placed at the tables.

The Casino. Mr. Kagan had a full piece of plywood cut and shaped like the top of a piano. It was painted black and it hung, inverted, from the top of the casino ceiling.

THE SHELDON HOUSE (1959)

The last building constructed, in 1959, was named the Sheldon House. Marilyn and Irwin Sheldon had loaned us $10,000 to defray the costs of its construction. The Sheldon House was lavish. Each room contained two double beds, a large closet, and a bathroom. The Sheldon House was built with a cellar where, among other things, extra double and single beds were kept. This became another venue in which Paul and Gary could cause mischief.

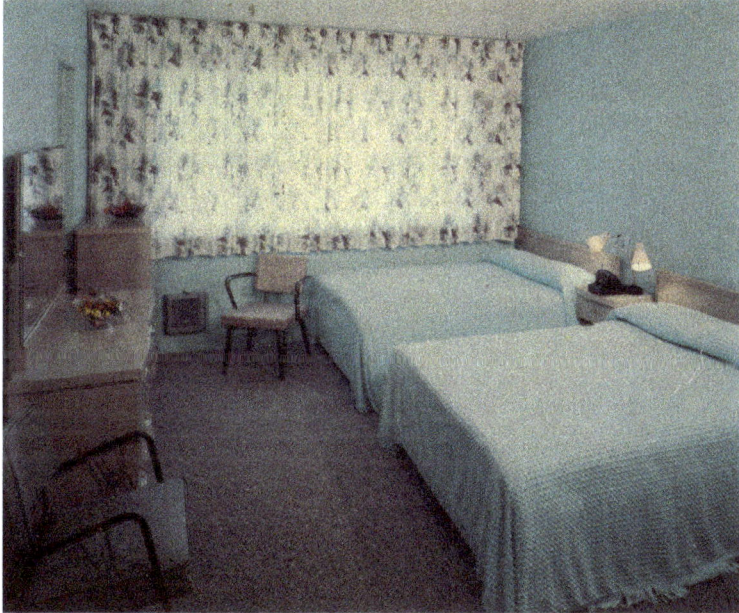

Bedroom in the Sheldon House

The Sheldon House contained 16 bedrooms. The law required that any new houses built at that time had to have a fire escape. Although adding this was expensive, it was done.

A GUEST'S TYPICAL DAY

Generally, guests vacationed at the hotel for either a week or just a weekend. A few stayed all summer and left after Labor Day. Regardless of how they traveled, guests generally arrived at the hotel Friday afternoon. In most cases, they were accompanied by a child. The

141

guest's first meal would be dinner. As the years progressed, most would invariably arrive by auto.

While the car was parked at the hotel's entrance, they registered. Most of the new arrivals had previously been at the hotel and the room in which they were to stay had been decided in advance. The bellhop drove the vehicle to the parking lot closest to their room and the guests walked to their room. The bellhop unloaded the luggage and brought it to the guest's room. The bellmen were very courteous, and they were never known to refuse a tip.

The Sheldon House

There were guests who had never been to Lesser Lodge. The price they were to pay for their lodging had previously been decided by phone or mail. These people were shown their room and in most cases they accepted the accommodations. If they did not care for the room, the hotel made every effort to please them. When everyone was satisfied, the bellhop went through his routine. Here, again, the bellman graciously accepted a tip.

At 8:00 a.m., children were brought by their parents to the head of the road that led to the day camp. The road to the camp was located adjacent to the main building. Counselors would lead the campers to the camp house for the ritual flag-raising and a healthy breakfast.

Every morning at 8:30, the hotel's loudspeakers would bark (sometimes in a heavy Polish accent) "Ladies and gentlemen, breakfast is now being served in zee main dining room." Since there was only one dining room, no one had difficulty finding it. But management felt it added a bit of prestige to specify that it was the "main" dining room. Some of the guests were such hardy eaters they would have found the dining room had it been located in a jungle.

After breakfast, many of the guests would go for a walk along Route 52 in order to help digest their meal. No matter how much the guest ate, their cost remained the same. Being above average in intelligence and weight, many took advantage of the no differential in cost.

The athletic director arranged various games and activities for the guests depending upon the weather. The guests could either participate in the activities provided by the athletic director or lounge around.

Then, at 1:00 p.m. the loudspeakers would bark again, "Ladies and gentlemen, lunch is now being served in the main dining room." This was one activity all the guests participated in.

The loudspeakers were also used to inform guests of an incoming telephone call; "Telephone call for Mr. Packman, please pick up a phone." There were "house" phones located in various places which were connected to the hotel switchboard. The switchboard operator would then connect the guest to the incoming call. The loudspeakers curtailed napping and kept the guests on their toes.

Outbound calling was an expensive proposition because the hotel added a surcharge onto the already high cost of the long distance call. A "person to person" call was one wherein the caller wasn't obliged to pay for the call if the person specified was not able to answer the phone. Many guests trying to "beat the system" would place calls person-to-person which contained a code such as a call placed to "Mr. Jacket." That would mean to bring my jacket when you drive up on Friday.

Every clear-weathered day, many guests went to the swimming pool to tan themselves. At times, the band played at the pool and the people danced. At other times, entertainers were hired to perform at the pool. Lou Goldstein, a tummler and jack-of-all-trades social director at Grossinger's for many years, would occasionally appear at the Lesser lodge telling jokes and performing his signature "Simon Sez" routine at the pool. On another day, it could be a Conga band. When there was no entertainment, there was a lot of horsing around. Cards and mah jongg were favorites and there might be five or more tables of guests playing at any given time in the afternoon.

While the adults enjoyed themselves, the children were at the day camp having a great time. They went to arts and crafts, enjoyed hay rides, and row boating, horseback riding, and so on. The counselors at the camp kept the children busy all day. Children would be taken to the pool twice a day for a swim. They would be left at the pool at 4:30 to meet their parents before dinner. At 6:30, the campers would again meet and be taken to the camp for dinner. At 8:30, campers and parents would meet outside of the main dining room.

The parents, knowing their children were well taken care of, enjoyed themselves. A mimeograph of the days' events looked like this:

The Lesser Lodge

WHITE SULPHUR SPRINGS
NEW YORK

ACTIVITIES
Saturday, July 4, 1959

MORNING
Breakfast	8:00 - 10:00
Nature walk with Noel	10:15 - Meet on main porch
Archery lessons with Shelly	10:30 - Along camp road
Chess tournament	10:30 - Card room
Tennis	11:00 - Tennis courts
Arts & Crafts with Bertie	11:30 - Art & Crafts Bldg.
Swimming lessons with Wally	11:45 - Pool

AFTERNOON
Lunch	1:00 - 2:00
Horseback Riding at Circle H Ranch	2:30 - Meet in Card room
Lesser's vs. Youngsville Inn	2:30 - Baseball Field
Simon Sez (prizes galore)	3:00 - Pool
Poolside Dancing	3:45 - Pool
Shopping in Liberty	See Charlie the Chauffeur

EVENING
Cocktail Hour - Main Lobby	6:30
Dinner	7:00 - 8:30
Fireworks	9:00 - Dock at Lake
Staff basketball(waiters v. counselors) under the lights	9:30 - Basketball Court

```
CASINO                              9:30

    The Polka Dots
    Buddy Hackett
Dancing to Leon Seaver and his Orchestra
```

One of the major highlights of the camp experience at Lesser's was called "night patrol." The counselors were assigned rooms to check, allowing the parents freedom to enjoy their evening activities without worrying. The counselors would check each room where there were young children and, if there was a problem, a child crying or uneasy, they would advise the parents. Since dinner started at 7:00 p.m., guests had an adequate amount of time to wash, change their clothing or perform other activities, depending on the age of the guest. For six evenings during the week, meat or chicken was served for dinner. On Sundays steak was served for lunch. Sunday was the day of departure and the hotel wanted the departing guests to leave with a good taste in their mouths.

Most of the guests were couples whose husbands stayed only for the weekend. The wives were free to luxuriate for the rest of the week. Each evening the wives and male guests would go to the Casino to dance and enjoy the fine entertainment provided by the hotel. Most of the waiters and busboys also went to the casino to enjoy the show and to dance with the wives. Dancing with the wives enhanced tips. The dancing continued after the show and then about 12:30 a.m. the guests were free to go to bed or to the card room where they had an additional opportunity to drink coffee, eat coffee cake and get fat.

David Auerbach (1957)

On Sundays the musicians would play music in the lobby. There was a large opening between the lobby and the dining room so that the music could be heard there as well. Often, one of the musicians would sing, or one of the guests would lend his or her voice for the entertainment of guests.

One day in 1957, as the musicians were taking a break, my six-year-old nephew, David Auerbach, my sister's son, sat down at the piano and started playing popular songs. He never had piano lessons and it was amazing how well he played. I stood in disbelief at what I was hearing.

The Event of the Century (1961)

My son Gary and my nephew Paul were born four days apart. It was decided to have their Bar Mitzvah at the Lesser Lodge. Preparations were always made for a Fourth of July opening, but this year, 1961, the preparations were made to open earlier.

My son had studied his Haftorah with reluctance—a great deal of reluctance. Each period we received his report card and each time he had an "F" next to all his subjects. When asked what the F stood for, he said, unhesitatingly, "Fair." One day the rabbi phoned my wife and told her he was kicking Gary out of Hebrew school. My wife asked, "How can you kick him out of school if he is doing fairly well in each subject." The rabbi then informed my wife that the *F* stood for "fail." But he learned his Haftorah. He memorized everything from a record we had to purchase.

*My son Gary and nephews Paul and David Auerbach lighting
candles at the Bar Mitzvah*

The entire family and many friends were invited to
spend the entire weekend at the Lesser Lodge to
celebrate Gary's and Paul's Bar Mitzvahs. There were
over 200 invitees, and the rooms they were to occupy
were decided by lottery. Among the people we invited
were all of our friends. The casino was opened and
entertainment was provided.

My father officiated at the Bar Mitzvah of his
grandchildren. They both *read* their Haftorah and my
father hardly winced.

It was a festive occasion. My cousins Jackie and
Shirley Murray found their bed halfway out the window
when they returned to their room.

Jack Stern, another cousin, attended the Bar Mitzvah, and he drank much too much Scotch whiskey. My brother was with Jack in the bathroom while Jack was throwing up, holding the toilet basin as if he was madly in love with it. At this moment, Jack's father walked into the bathroom. Without a moment's hesitation my brother said, "Jack, say hello to Dad."

Unknown to anyone, Gary and Paul decided to sip the wine that had been placed on every table. They spent their Bar Mitzvah night flat on their backs, sleeping. But a good time was had by all, except Gary and Paul.

WEEPING WILLOWS (1962)

During 1962, I purchased 20 small weeping willow trees. I planted them, half bordering the lake and the other half near the day camp and pool. When I last saw them, they were huge and majestic.

LIGHTNING STRIKES

Two years after the Bar Mitzvah, as we were preparing the fully booked hotel for the Passover holidays, the main house—the heart of the hotel—was engulfed in fire. This was on March 28, 1963, at about 3:00 a.m.

Firemen pumped water from the lake.[41] Two fire companies fought the fire for over six hours, but to no avail. That same night, the Ambassador Hotel, near Fallsburg, also lost its main building in a fire.[42]

Following the fire, my father sold the property and paid off all the bills. Several years after my mother's death in 1957, my father remarried and moved to Florida.

My son, Gary, became a lawyer, was a Tax Law Specialist with the Internal Revenue Service, had various positions on Wall Street, and now consults on retirement plan matters and writes educational books for the American Institute of Certified Public Accountants and Aspen Publishers.[43]

My nephew Paul lives in Middletown New York with his wife Diana. Paul and Diana own and operate *Total Green*, designing and installing renewable energy systems for residential and commercial systems.[44] Paul has three children.

My nephew David is a teacher and heads up the Science Department at the very prestigious Cardigan Mountain School in Canaan, New Hampshire.[45] David and his wife Suzanne have a son and a daughter.

My niece Jill Lesser lives in Brooklyn with her husband Jeff. Jill was a pre-school teacher at a private school in Brooklyn for 18 years.

I became a commercial real estate broker and an accountant. I sold my accounting practice when I was 65 years old and moved to Florida. Evelyn and I are still active and have a wonderful social life going to the doctors every day. Last year, for my 89th birthday, my son and I wrote a self-help book called *Basic Accounting Simplified*.[46] The book has been well received, is selling well, was honored with an award, and has gotten good reviews.[47]

AN ERA ENDS

Air conditioning was a significant factor leading to the downfall of many hotels in the Catskills. People who had air conditioning in their homes no longer had need of the cooler weather found in the Catskills.

Inexpensive airfare to far-off places also caused a dwindling of the number of people wishing to vacation in the Catskills.

All of the hotel owners prayed that gambling would be legalized in the Catskills, thinking that would lead to a rejuvenation of the area, but it was never to be. Slowly but surely, one by one, the area's hotels and rooming houses were forced out of business.

At one time, there were thousands of hotels and rooming houses in the Catskills. Now the number can be counted on the fingers of the hands.

Yes, an era had ended. But oh, what an era it had been.

The End

APPENDIX A

ADDITIONAL PICTURES

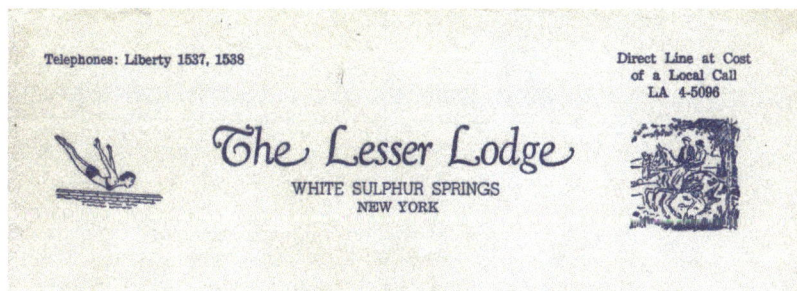

Telephones: Liberty 1537, 1538

Direct Line at Cost
of a Local Call
LA 4-5096

The Lesser Lodge
WHITE SULPHUR SPRINGS
NEW YORK

Letterhead showing new direct telephone line to hotel

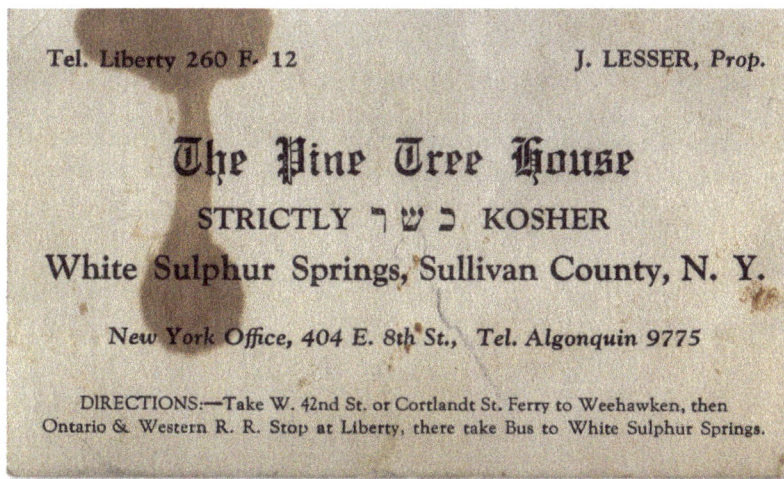

Tel. Liberty 260 F. 12

J. LESSER, Prop.

The Pine Tree House

STRICTLY כ ש ר KOSHER

White Sulphur Springs, Sullivan County, N. Y.

New York Office, 404 E. 8th St., Tel. Algonquin 9775

DIRECTIONS:—Take W. 42nd St. or Cortlandt St. Ferry to Weehawken, then
Ontario & Western R. R. Stop at Liberty, there take Bus to White Sulphur Springs.

My father's original business card before renaming property to "Lesser Lodge"

A Vacation for the Entire Family

THE LESSER LODGE
**WHITE SULPHUR SPRINGS
NEW YORK
Tel. Liberty 1537-8**

SCHEDULE

OF RATES

EFFECTIVE JUNE 27—SEASON 1954

ACCOMMODATIONS AND RATES
EFFECTIVE JUNE 27—SEASON 1954
ALL RATES ARE PER PERSON AND
FOR ACCOMMODATIONS TO SHARE

	Weekly—Rooms for 2
Hillside Bungalow	$52.50
Main Bungalow	55.00—$57.50

MAIN BUILDING

Second Floor	55.00— 57.50
First Floor	60.00
New Annex	60.00

New Annex—

Private bath or shower	67.50— 70.00
Brand New—De-Luxe Building	75.00

All corner rooms are $2.50 more per person than rates quoted for those rooms.

Bills are pro-rated after week's stay

Children—$45. Deluxe—$50.—$52.50.

July & August Daily Rates—$10. Deluxe (Private Bath)—$12.—$13.

June Rates from $37.50 per person

Children from $25.00 per person

Reservations are not definite until confirmed and must be accompanied by a $10.00 deposit per person.

Free Golf and Boating

RESERVATION FORM

●

Name...

Address...

....

Telephone...

Number in party...

Date of arrival...

Date of Departure...

Accommodations 1st choice...

2nd choice...

3rd choice...

_____

TEAR OFF AND RETURN WITH DEPOSIT

Picture key:[48]

A room in Sheldon House, which at the time of the hotel's demise rented for $100 a week. The room was considerably larger than shown in the photograph. (*Top left*)

The Card Room. The card room was dramatic in appearance and comfort. The guests enjoyed playing poker, bridge, and other games. (*Bottom left*)

The Main Dining Room. Only a portion of the dining room is shown. Ultimately the dining room was able to seat over 270 guests. (*Top right*)

The Lobby shown from dining room. This was the last lobby. (*Bottom right*)

Picture key:

The Sheldon House was the last house constructed. It was built on the land previously occupied by the barn and was quite an improvement. (*Top left*)

The swimming pool on a sunny day. (*Top right*)

Dock overlooking lake. The row boats were tied to the dock. (*Bottom left*)

Handball, basketball, and volley ball courts. The day camp and some of the staff quarters were located behind the handball courts. (*Bottom right*)

Claire and Seymour Lesser and Marilyn Auerbach Lesser (1946)

Herb Auerbach points out to a guest the beauties of the hotel on the walkway between the Alsyn and Marilyn Houses

Dorothy and Harold Caplan my wife's parents, me, and my parents,
Sara and Joseph Lesser

Me, Mom, and Seymour in front of the eight-room bungalow

Irving and Jeannette Sewitt, season regulars, in front of the Casino/Playhouse (circa 1958)

Lesser Lodge, Inc. Stock Certificate (1944)

PFC Alvin Lesser (1946)

My sister Marilyn on swings in front of barn (1940s). At her right-hand elbow is the eight-room bungalow

Badminton (circa 1949)

Seymour's wife Claire, my sister Marilyn, and wife Evelyn (circa 1955)

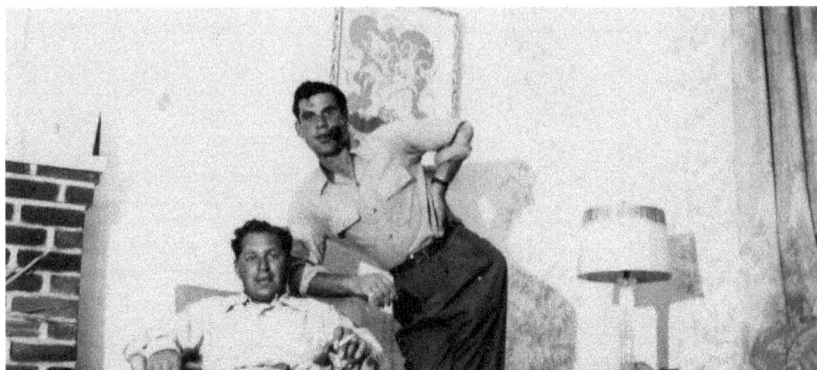

Seymour Lesser and my sister's husband Herbert Auerbach (circa 1950)

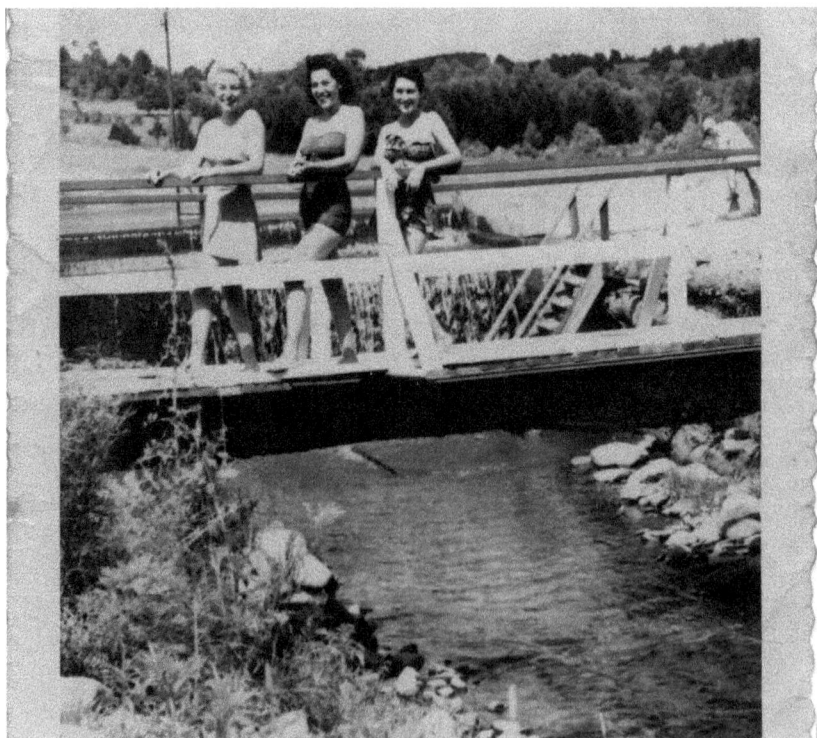

Unknown guests on wooden bridge over stream beneath dam leading to beach area

Main Street looking West, Liberty, New York

My Brother Seymour, my mother Sara Lesser, and Me (circa 1944)

My wife Evelyn Lesser with Gina Miles (circa 1960s)

Marilyn Auerbach (circa 1940s)

Boat dock. handball courts and day camp shown in background

View of Lesser Lake alongside Route 52

Jill Lesser, Gary Lesser, Joseph Lesser, and Paul Auerbach – Bar Mitzvah (1961). Don't let Gary and Paul fool you with their innocent faces at their Bar Mitzvah. They caused plenty of trouble before and after they became men.

My sister Marilyn Auerbach, Audrey Donnenfeld (friend), my wife Evelyn, Gina and Jack Miles, me, Herb Donnenfeld, and Herbert Auerbach., We were all so young and happy. Now there are only three of us left.

Marilyn Lesser Auerbach and my mother Sarah Lesser (circa 1940)

Me, an unknown girlfriend, with Irving Cohen, former maître d' at Concord Hotel, piano player and children's waiter at the Lesser Lodge (circa 1937)

Lawn between Casino (left) and eight-room bungalow (right).

My parents, Sara and Joseph Lesser

My brother Seymour and an unknown guest (circa 1940)

APPENDIX B

THE "GREAT PATENT" AND OTHER DEEDS

THE "GREAT PATENT"

All of the land in Sullivan County and parts of Ulster and Delaware counties in New York belonged to Nanisinos, a chief of the Esopus Indians. In 1707, Nanisinos sold an immense tract of land (2 million acres) to Johannes Hardenburgh (Hardenbergh), a merchant, for the sum of 60 pounds. Johannes Hardenburgh was born in Albany, New York in 1670. In 1690, he was High Sheriff of Ulster County. Hardenburgh served as a Major in the Ulster County Regiment and was knighted by Queen Anne on the recommendation of the Duke of Marlborough for gallantry at the decisive battle of Blenheim in Queen Anne's War (1702-1713).

The purchase was subsequently confirmed and a land patent—that has become known as the "Great Patent" —was granted to Hardenburgh and six others on April 20, 1708. There were disputes as to whether Hardenburgh's acquisition of the property had been truly legal. Over the next 40 years, the make-up of the owners changed substantially due to deaths and sales. A few years after Hardenburgh's death, the patent was divided into "Great Lots" in 1749 and apportioned among the owners. These lots were further subdivided into tracts and divisions of various sizes. Shares in the patent changed hands frequently, and the terms under which the land was sold or leased were so varied and complex that it impeded settlement of the district and clouded the title to most of the tracts until well after the American Revolution.

The Lesser Lodge was located in subdivision 36, in division number 12, of Great Lot No. 2 of the Hardenburgh Patent.

SOURCES AND RELATED INFORMATION—

- Index of the property that was part of the Hardenburgh and other patents inherited by Nicholas Elmendorf from Lucas and William H. Elmendorf of Kingston (Ulster County), New York. The index shows lot numbers, deed numbers, dates, original owners and their heirs, family members, subdivision numbers, and lot sizes. The earliest deed recorded is dated 1792. NY State Archives, see *http://www.archives.nysed.gov/g/vrc/environm ent/find/88_0049.shtml#overview.*

- James Eldridge Quinlan, History of Sullivan County: Embracing an Account of its Geology, Climate, Aborigines, Early Settlement, Organization; The Formation of its Towns, With Biographical Sketches of Prominent Residents, G. M. Reebe and W. T. Morgans, Liberty, NY (1873). Available at *http://books.google.com* (search for "Sullivan County").

- Background Information on the Hardenburgh Patent, Delaware County, NY, available at *www.dcnyhistory.org/hardenburghpatentbobbo yd.html.*

- See Historical Maps, The Livingston Manor, NY Quadrangle, available at *http://historical.mytopo.com/quad.cfm?quadna me=Livingston%20Manor&state=NY&series=15,* Choose "Southeast" quadrangle jpeg. Pan to just below "L" in Liberty on map to see Shingle Brook at State Route (SR) 52.

- The Delaware County NY Genealogy and History Site contains public domain records for genealogical research in Delaware County, NY, visit them at *http://www.dcnyhistory.org/*.

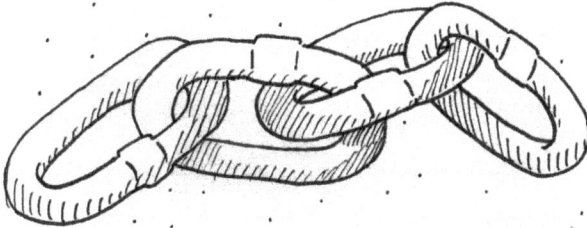

CHAIN OF DEEDS

There were numerous conveyances of very large tracts in the 1700s. As time went on, the acreage conveyed got less and less. In 1864, the track size was 109 acres. Deeds earlier than 1864 were not searched. Deeds in the chain after 1864 are as follows:

Lefever to Kimball. The earliest deed in the chain is in 1864, from Newton Lefever of Rosedale in Ulster County, New York to William D. Kimball of Liberty for $684. [Liber 48 at page 281.] It is for 109 acres and encompasses all of lot 36 in Divisions 11 and 12 of Great Lot 2 of the Hardenburgh Patent.

Note. The property that became the Lesser Lodge (Liber 31) was part of this tract.

Kimball to Wood. The deed from William and Deborah Kimball of Liberty, New York to William Wood of Liberty for $1,100 is for 50 acres off the south part of lot 36 which is the property that becomes part of the Lesser Lodge. That 50-acre description remains the same for the rest of the chain. [Liber 76 at page 508.]

A summary of subsequent deeds in the Lesser Lodge property chain are as follows:

Wood to Barnhart. On April 5, 1902, William and Melissa Wood of Liberty, New York conveyed the property to Arthur Barnhart, of Liberty for $1,800. [Liber 131 at page 53.]

Barnhart to Wood. On June 11, 1004, Arthur and Lavinnie Barnhart conveyed the property to William and Melissa Wood of Liberty, New York for $250. [Liber 143 at page 635.]

Wood to Kratz. On February 18, 1909, William and Melissa Wood conveyed the property to Henry Kratz of Callicoon, New York for $2,000. [Liber 164 at page 454.]

Kratz to Krongel. On December 20, 1920, Henry and Rosie Kratz of Liberty, New York conveyed the property to Bessie Krongel of 242 Delancy Street, New York City for $1. [Liber 206 at page 333.]

Krongel to Eisen. On June 3, 1922, Bessie Krongel of Liberty, New York conveyed the property to Celia Eisen of 126 Scholes Street, Brooklyn, New York for $4,500. [Liber 218 at page 510]

Note. Celia Eisen conveyed one acre of the property to the Trustees of Common School

District No. 7 for $1 on August 25, 1922. [Liber 221 at page 135] This conveyance is reflected as an exception and reservation in the subsequent chain of title.

Eisen to Lesser. Celia Eisen, Isreal Fox, and Regina Fox of White Sulphur Springs, NY, granted the property to Joseph Lesser of Ferndale, New York for $5,400 on July 12, 1923. [Liber 228 at page 89.]

Joseph Lesser and Sarah Lesser to Lesser Lodge, Inc. On July 3, 1944, the property was conveyed to the hotel for $1. [Liber 384 at page 63.]

Lesser Lodge to Camp Deer Path, Inc. On February 26, 1964, the property was conveyed to Camp Deer Path of Spring Valley, New York. [Liber 669 at page 481.]

Camp Deer Path, Inc. to Camp Omnibus Incorporated. On October 7, 1966, the property was conveyed to Camp Omnibus of Goshen, New York. [Liber 708 at page 594.]

Camp Omnibus Incorporated to Silver Masque Players, Inc. On September 22, 1976, the property was conveyed to Silver Masque Players, a theatre group from Brooklyn, New York. [Liber 838 at page 275.]

STATE ROUTE 52

Prior to 1952, New York State Route 52 ran along some old town highways and a former plank road that ran from Liberty to Jeffersonville (see maps later in this Appendix). In 1952, the Department of

Transportation began a process of purchasing lands to reroute SR 52 to eliminate a curve east of Midway Road (shown as dashed line on map). Final maps were filed in 1954, and reconstruction lasting several years to realign portions of old SR 52 between Liberty and Jeffersonville commenced.

MIDWAY ROAD

In 1962, Shingle Brook Road was lengthened from 2.00 miles to 2.09 miles so that it could be reconnected to SR 52. When new SR 52 was constructed sometime between 1955 and 1961 to the south of the old alignment, they had to tie Shingle Brook Road back into the new SR 52 so they used the old alignment of SR 52 as a way to lengthen Shingle and then "T'd" that out to the new SR 52, thereby increasing its length by 0.9 mile. In 1965, Shingle Brook was renamed Midway Road.

If you turned right at the end of Shingle Brook Road, you would have been on old SR 52, which was formerly an old town highway (TH 80). You would have crossed Shingle Brook heading west toward its intersection with Hector Road. The bed of that road is still visible on the aerial map but the road is abandoned and the bridge is gone.

If you turned left at the end of Shingle Brook Road you would have headed east on old SR 52.

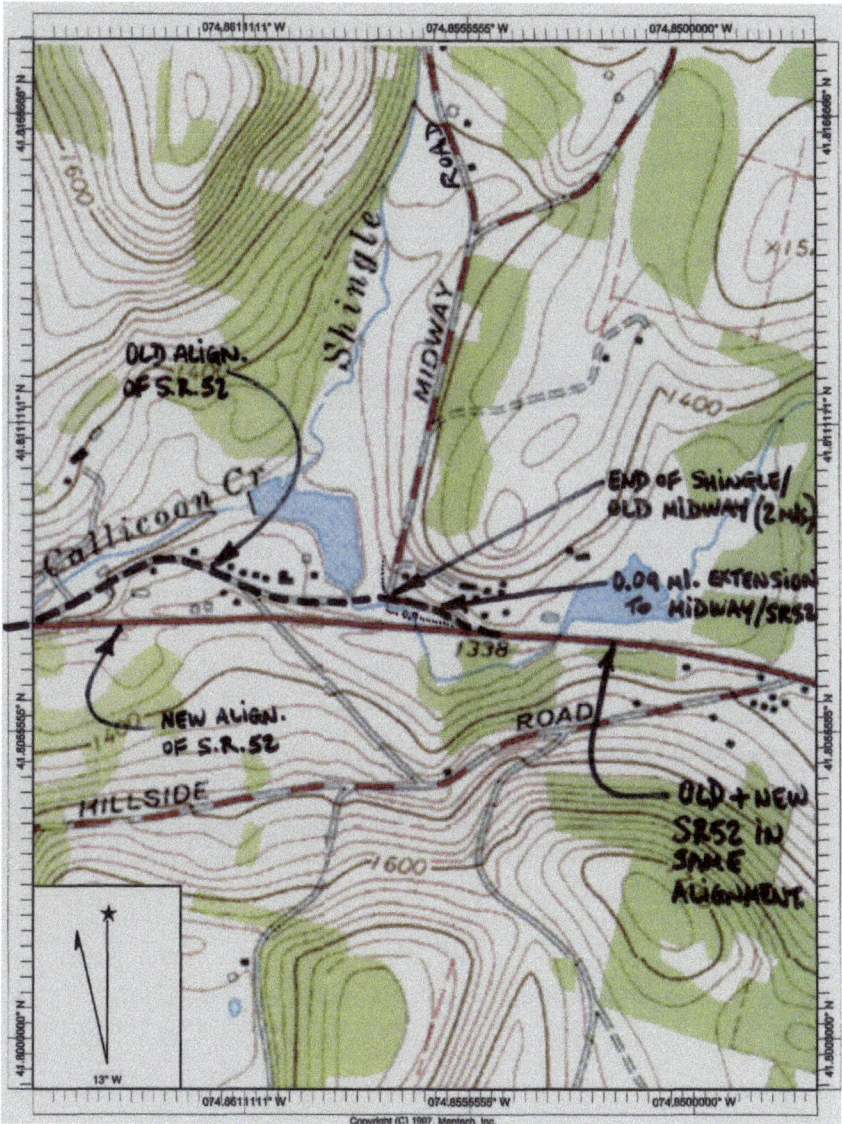

Source: Map and descriptions provided by Dermot P. Dowd LS, Sullivan County Division of Public Works (D.P.W.), Civil Engineer.

The Lesser Lodge was located between Midway Road and Lesser Lake (shown to the right). The stream connecting the two lakes is shown. Image available at:

http://maps.google.com/maps?ll=41.808877,-74.854789&spn=0.005086,0.01811&t=m&z=16&vpsrc=6&lci=com.panoramio.all

Lesser Lodge (main building):
41°48'28.23N, 74°51'19.26W

Midway School:
41°48'29.60N, 74°51'26.60W

APPENDIX C

ADDITIONAL RESOURCES

Catskill Internet Links

The Catskills Institute, Brown University, available at *Http://www.brown.edu/Research/Catskills_Institute*.

Rise and Fall of the Borscht Belt, documentary about the Borscht Belt; directed and produced by *Peter Davis*, available at *http://www.villonfilms.com/filmrec.php?queryIndex=23 &director=1*.

New York New Jersey Trail Conference, connecting people with nature, visit them at *http://www.nynjtc.org*.

The Sullivan County Democrat, newspaper and archives, Callicoon, NY, available at *http://www.sc-democrat.com/index_news.htm*.

The Catskill Chronicle newspaper, available at *http://thecatskillchronicle.com*.

Purple Mountain Press, books about New York State and maritime books, visit them at *http://www.catskill.net/purple/*.

Liberty Museum & Arts Center, 46 South Main Street, Liberty, New York 12754 (845) 292-2394. See *http://www.libertymuseum.com/history.html*.

Historical and Reference Materials

F.W. Beers, *County Atlas of Sullivan*, New York, Walker and Jewett, New York (1875).

Esterita "Cissie" Blumberg, *Remember the Catskills: A Hotelkeeper's Story*, Purple Mountain Press (1996).

Phil Brown, *In the Catskills: A Century of the Jewish Experience in "The Mountains,"* Columbia University Press, New York, NY (2002).

Phil Brown, *Catskill Culture: A Mountain Rat's Memories of the Great Jewish Resort Area*, Temple University Press, Philadelphia, PA (1998).

John Conway, *Dutch Shultz and His Lost Catskills' Treasure*, Purple Mountain Press, Ltd., Fleischmanns, NY (2010).

John Conway, *Remembering the Sullivan County Catskills*, Purple Mountain Press, Ltd., Fleischmanns, NY (2008); compiled from the best of John Conway's popular "Retrospect" columns.

John Conway, *Retrospect: An Anecdotal History of Sullivan County, New York,* Purple Mountain Press, Ltd., Fleischmanns, NY (1996).

John Conway, *Sullivan County (NY): A Bicentennial History in Images*, The History Press, Charleston, SC (2009).

John Conway, *Blessed By The Gods*, Catskill-Delaware Press, Callicoon, NY (2012).

Myrna Katz Frommer and Harvey Frommer, *It Happened in the Catskills: An Oral History in the Words of Busboys, Bellhops, Guests, Proprietors, Comedians, Agents, and Others Who Lived It*, State University of New York Press, NY (2009).

Stefan Kanfer, *A Summer World: The Attempt to Build a Jewish Eden in the Catskills, from the Days of the Ghetto to the Rise and Decline of the Borscht Belt*, Farrar, Straus & Giroux, New York, NY (1989).

David Gold, *The River and The Mountains*, Library Research Associates (1997).

Richard Grossinger, *Out of Babylon: Ghosts of Grossinger's*, Frog, Ltd., Berkeley, CA (1997).

Tania Grossinger, *Growing Up at Grossinger's*, Skyhorse Publishing (2008).

Irwin Richman, *Borscht Belt Bungalows: Memoirs Of Catskill Summers*, Temple University Press, Philadelphia, PA (1998).

James Quinlan, *History of Sullivan County*, James Quinlan, G.M. Beebe & W.T. Morgans, Liberty, New York (1873).

Robert Titus, *The Catskills in the Ice Age*, revised edition, Purple Mountain Press, Ltd., Fleischmanns, NY (2003).

Robert Titus, *The Catskills: A Geological Guide*, revised 3rd edition, The Purple Mountain Press, Ltd (2004).

Robert Titus, *The Other Side of Time, Essays by "The Catskill Geologist*," The Purple Mountain Press, Ltd (2007).

Manville B. Wakefield, *To The Mountains by Rail*, 1st Edition, Wakefield Press, Grahamsville, NY (1970).

APPENDIX D

WHITE SULPHUR SPRINGS HOTELS

Barsalee Country Club
Beck's Villa
Eagle's Nest
Happiness House (became Tel Aviv Hotel)
Hotel Leona (Fischer)
Lawrence House
Lesser Lodge (formerly The Pine Tree House)
Pinehurst Manor
Rose Cottages Hotel
Royal Acres
Victoria
White Sulphur Springs House
Willi Farm House

APPENDIX E

BORSCHT BELT
ACTORS & PERFORMERS

Comedians who got their start or regularly performed in Catskill resorts include:

Al Bernie	Freddie Roman
Alan King	Fyvush Finkel
Allan Sherman	Gene Wilder
Bea Arthur	George Burns and
Benny Bell	Gracie Allen
Betty Garrett	George Gobel
Bill Dana	George Jessel
Buddy Hackett	Gertrude Berg
Carl Reiner	Groucho Marx
Charlie Manna	Harpo Marx
Charlotte Rae	Harvey Korman
Chico Marx	Henny Youngman
Danny Kaye	Jack Benny
Don Rickles	Jack Carter
Eddie Cantor	Jack E. Leonard
Estelle Getty	Jack Gilford
Fanny Brice	Jackie Mason

Jackie Vernon	Mort Sahl
Jackie Wakefield	Myron Cohen
Jan Murray	Pesach Burstein
Jean Carroll	Peter Sellers
Jerry Lewis	Phil Silvers
Joan Rivers	Phyllis Diller
Joey Adams	Red Buttons
Joey Bishop	Robert Klein
Jonathan Winters	Rodney Dangerfield
Lenny Bruce	Rowan & Martin
Lou Menchell	Sam Levenson
Mal Lawrence	Shecky Greene
Mansel Rubenstein	Shelley Berman
Marty Allen	Sid Caesar
Marty Gale	Totie Fields
Mel Brooks	Victor Borga
Mickey Katz	Woody Allen
Milton Berle	Zero Mostel
Morey Amsterdam	

There were also a large number of actors, singers, dancers, magicians, clowns, musicians and other variety acts including:

Abbe Lane	Eddie Fisher
Al Jolson	Emmett Kelly
Barbra Streisand	Eydie Gormé
Benny Fields	Greta Garbo
Blossom Seeley	Joel Grey
Benny Goodman	John Barrymore
Beryl Wallace	Kitty Carlisle
Bobby Van	Larry Schwalb
Carole King	Lesley Gore
David Rose	Libby Holman
Dinah Shore	Lillian Roth

Mae Questel
Maxie Rosenbloom
Mel Tormé
Mimi Benzell
Mitch Miller
Moss Hart
Neil Sedaka
Oscar Levant
Peg-Leg Bates

Rick Saphire
Shari Lewis
Sophie Tucker
Steve Lawrence
Tina Louise
Tony Martin
Van Johnson
Walter Winchel

Emmett Kelly the clown is shown with Larry "Houdini" Schwalb, a former
Catskill Mountain resort magician. Larry is currently a
television personality and a professional safecracker at Houdini Lock &
Safe Company in Philadelphia.

George Jessel, 1st VP, and Eddie Cantor, President, Jewish Theatrical Guild

ENDNOTES

[1] With his family, Don vacationed in the Catskills during the `50s and early `60s until he went off on his own in 1964 – to work as a musician with his rock band "The Abstracts" at the Gilbert Hotel in South Fallsburg. The group is best known for their now-classic recording "Always Always" released in 1965 and for their recent (2011) album *"Hey Let's Go Now!"* See *http://www.60sgaragebands.com/abstracts.html.*

[2] Originally named Robertsonville (and was sometimes referred to as "Robinsonville"). The town was originally settled in 1800 and named for Bradley Robertson, according to John Conway. Name was changed in 1890, per Delbert E. VanEtten, Town Historian. See *http://www.betweenthelakes.com/NY/sullivan/sullivan_p lacenames.htm.*

[3] Town of Liberty was formed from the *Town of Lumberland* on March 13, 1807.

[4] See *Terraserver* topological map of area at (center) *http://www.terraserver.com/view.asp?cx=512143&cy=46 28486&proj=32618&mpp=2.5&pic=map&prov=dg2&stac= 8151&ovrl=-1&drwl=-1.* See, 1923 historical maps of Livingston Manor, NY Quadrangle, available at *http://historical.mytopo.com/quad.cfm?quadname=Livin gston%20Manor&state=NY&series=15* (located in SE portion of quadrangle).

[5] The "Catskill Mountains" extends northwest of New York City and southwest of Albany.

[6] News from Brown, The Brown University News Bureau (November 29, 1995, available at

http://www.brown.edu/Administration/News_Bureau/19 95-96/95-062i.html.

[7] See, e.g., John Conway, *Blessed By The Gods*, Purple Mountain Press Ltd., Fleishmanns, NY (2012), discusses how early physicians discovered some near magical properties in the Sullivan County air that provided miraculous improvement in those suffering from pulmonary ailments, and how decades later this same curative air was the basis of the rest cure dispensed by dozens of tuberculosis treatment facilities, including the world famous Loomis Sanitarium.

[8] John Conway, *Loomis: The Man, The Sanitarium, and the Search for the Cure*, available at *http://www.catskill.net/purple/loomis.htm.*

[9] Postcard available at Card Cow, see *http://www.cardcow.com.* See also, Nathan Mayberg, *Loomis Sanitarium is on Their Mind* (June 7, 2005), available at *http://www.sc-democrat.com/archives/2005/news/06June/07/loomis.htm.*

[10] Joseph Lesser (1889-1966) was born in Bobowa, Austria/Poland. He was 21 years old when he immigrated to the United States from Holland in 1910.

[11] Sarah Lesser (1895-1957) was born in Bobowa, Austria/Poland.

[12] See, Don Markstein's Toonopedia , available at *http://www.toonopedia.com/katzen.htm.*

[13] Liberty Museum & Arts Center, see *http://www.libertymuseum.com/history.html.*

[14] The Delaware Lackawanna Railroad.

[15] The hotel was briefly called "The Pine Tree House" before being renamed the Lesser Lodge.

[16] See *Terraserver* topological map of area at *http://www.terraserver.com/view.asp?cx=512143&cy=46 28486&proj=32618&mpp=2.5&pic=map&prov=dg2&stac= 8151&ovrl=-1&drwl=-1.*

[17] Between the Lakes Group, recovering local history: "Betty DeWitt Coleman notes that the Lesser Lodge, a "Borscht Circuit" resort of some prominence, was just east of the old school....Susan Bielefeld relates that when her father removed the shingles from an old building he had purchased, on the layer beneath was painted "The Midway School" and "Bergman." She believes that the school building may have been used for staff housing for the resort, which also may have been known as "Kramer's." See *http://www.betweenthelakes.com/NY/sullivan/sullivan_p lacenames.htm*, use Ctrl+F keys and search for "Midway."

[18] "Brother, Can You Spare a Dime," lyrics by Yip Harburg, music by Jay Gorney (1931).

[19] The Leon Seaver Orchestra—Leon Seaver, saxaphone and clarinet; Mike Regal, drummer; Paul James, piano; and Sunny Radick, singer.

[20] Born Joseph Levitch, (1926).

[21] Born Yacov Moshe Maza (1936).

[22] Born David Daniel Kaminsky (1913-1987).

[23] Leonard Hacker in (1924-2003).

[24] Camp Chic-A-Lac, Youngsville, see *http://www.chicalac.com/*

[25] Morris and Molly Bergman were Russian immigrants who came to the U.S. through Ellis Island in the early 1900's. They owned a laundry business on Coney Island. The Bergmans had four children, Julius, Alex, Nathaniel (Alexis's father), and Ida (Skippy).

[26] See *http://citynoise.org/article/2078/in/brooklyn@ny* and *http://citynoise.org/noise/ben_and_sol_deli.*

27 A *shofar* is a trumpet made from a ram's horn that is used as a musical instrument for Jewish religious purposes. It is an extremely difficult instrument to play (i.e., that is to make any sound whatsoever).

28 The *Haftorah* is a short selection from the Prophets read on every Sabbath in a Jewish synagogue following a reading from the *Torah* (the first five books of the Jewish biblical canon; Genesis, Exodus, Leviticus, Numbers and Deuteronomy. The *Torah* is known in Christianity as the Pentateuch.

29 *Deuteronomy 14:3-10*: "Do not eat any detestable thing. These are the animals you may eat: the ox, the sheep, the goat, the deer, the gazelle, the roe deer, the wild goat, the ibex, the antelope and the mountain sheep. You may eat any animal that has a split hoof divided in two and that chews the cud. However, of those that chew the cud or that have a split hoof completely divided you may not eat the camel, or the rabbit. Although they chew the cud, they do not have a split hoof; they are ceremonially unclean for you. The pig is also unclean; although it has a split hoof, it does not chew the cud. You are not to eat their meat or touch their carcasses. Of all the creatures living in the water, you may eat any that has fins and scales. But anything that does not have fins and scales you may not eat; for you it is unclean;" *Exodus 23:19, Exodus 34:26, and Deuteronomy 14:21*: "Do not cook a young goat in its mother's milk;" see also *Kosher and Halal*, available at *http://meat.tamu.edu/kosher.html.*

30 Ritual slaughter is known as "shechitah" (pronounced sheh-KHEE-taw), and the person who performs the slaughter is called a "shochet (pronounced SHOW-khet)," both from the Hebrew root Shin-Chet-Tav, meaning to destroy or kill (slaughter). The method of slaughter is a single, quick, deep stroke across the throat with a perfectly sharp blade with no nicks or unevenness. This method is painless, causes unconsciousness within two seconds, and is

widely recognized as the most humane method of slaughter possible. Another advantage of shechitah is that it ensures more rapid draining of the blood, which is also necessary to make the meat kosher. The shochet is not simply a butcher; he must also be well-trained in the laws of ritual slaughter.

[31] When the Israelites departed from ancient Egypt, they left in great haste. As a result, they could note bake their bread in the usual manner because dough needed time to rise and for the bread to become leavened. The product of the leavening process is called "chametz" (pronounced ka-mets). In order to relive the experience of our ancestors, Jews may not own, eat, or benefit from *chametz* during Passover.

During the eight days of the Passover, Jews use only products that are free of *chametz*. *Matzah* is eaten during the holiday in order to experience the haste of our forefathers when they went forth from slavery to freedom. The punishment for eating chametz on Passover is the divine punishment of *kareth* (spiritual excision), one of the most severe levels of punishment in Judaism. There are numerous offenses punishable by *kareth. (See, http://en.wikipedia.org/wiki/Kareth.)*

In addition to not using chametz products during the festival, the use of dishes and utensils which have been used all year round with chametz is to be avoided. For that reason it is necessary to have two additional sets of dishes for Passover use. There are certain types of utensils that can, however, be ritually (kashered) for Passover use. Those items include:

• Pots and metal utensils without wooden handles. They must first be cleansed thoroughly and then allowed to stand unused for 24 hours. Then they must be completely immersed in boiling water. Glued items and items that cannot be cleansed thoroughly (such as a sieve) cannot be kashered for Passover. Larger pots or kettles may be kashered by first cleansing them as above and then filling them with water to the very top, allowing the water to boil and then placing a hot iron or stone inside the pot so that the boiling water runs over and down the sides of the pot.

• Glasses and glass plates which have not been used for hot liquids or solids during the year may be kashered for Passover by immersing them in cold water for a period of three days prior to Passover. Glass utensils (such as Pyrex) which are used with meat must be treated as china and cannot be kashered.

• Every part of the stove and oven must be thoroughly cleaned with a chemical cleanser and then allowed to stand for 24 hours or more without being used. The top range and the oven must then be heated.

The rules are interpreted differently depending upon the authority. Consult your Rabbi. See, e.g., *http://judaism.about.com/library/3_howto/ht_kosher.ht m* and *http://www.oukosher.org/index.php/passover/article/kas hering/*.

32 *Exodus 23:19, Exodus 34:26, Deuteronomy 14:21:* "Do not cook a young goat in its mother's milk." These passages have been interpreted as meaning that meat and dairy cannot be eaten together. This separation includes not only the foods themselves, but the utensils, pots and pans with which they are cooked, the plates and flatware from which they are eaten, the dishwashers or dishpans in which they are cleaned, and the towels on which they are dried.

33 See *http://Grossinger'sgolf.net.*

34 See *http://en.wikipedia.org/wiki/Red_Apple_Rest.*

35 See American Tap Dance Foundation, Tap Dance Hall of Fame; available at

http://www.atdf.org/awards/pegleg.html; and video at *http://www.youtube.com/watch?v=hauM4B7hcBQ*.

³⁶ Marilyn Lesser Auerbach, 1927-1993.

³⁷ See *http://ineedattention.com/pines/*; see Pines video at *http://vimeo.com/20260931*.

³⁸ Lesser Lake was fed by Horseshoe Brook and Shingle Brook. Ping-Pong Island was the area located in between these two streams on the southeastern edge of the property.

³⁹ See *http://www.basicaccountingsimplified.com*.

⁴⁰ The Quonset hut is a prefabricated shelter modeled after the World War I Nissen hut and used during World War II. The original huts were 16 feet in diameter with steel arch frames.

⁴¹ The firemen from the surrounding fire departments frequently tested their hoses, nozzles, and other equipment on the shores of Lesser Lake, which was only about 100 feet from Route 52. The lake provided the water and the firemen provided some entertainment for the guests to watch. It was very pretty to watch the fountains of water and the rainbows that were created on a sunny day.

⁴² Two Sullivan County Hotels Burned Last Thursday Morning, *Sullivan County Democrat*, Vol. LXXI, pages 1 and 5, Callicoon, NY (reported in the weekly edition on April 4, 1963).

⁴³ See *http://www.garylesser.com*.

⁴⁴ See *http://totalgreenus.com*.

⁴⁵ See *http://www.cardigan.org*.

⁴⁶ See *http://www.basicaccountingsimplified.com*.

⁴⁷ See *http://www.basicaccountingsimplified.com/BAS-press.pdf*.

⁴⁸ Postcard pictures were photographed by Max Schwartz Printing.